ONCE UPON A RHYME

IMAGINATION FOR A NEW GENERATION

Cheshire

Edited by Steve Twelvetree

 Young**Writers**

First published in Great Britain in 2004 by:
Young Writers
Remus House
Coltsfoot Drive
Peterborough
PE2 9JX
Telephone: 01733 890066
Website: www.youngwriters.co.uk

SB ISBN 1 84460 429 2

Foreword

Young Writers was established in 1991 and has been passionately devoted to the promotion of reading and writing in children and young adults ever since. The quest continues today. Young Writers remains as committed to engendering the fostering of burgeoning poetic and literary talent as ever.

This year's Young Writers competition has proven as vibrant and dynamic as ever and we are delighted to present a showcase of the best poetry from across the UK. Each poem has been carefully selected from a wealth of *Once Upon A Rhyme* entries before ultimately being published in this, our twelfth primary school poetry series.

Once again, we have been supremely impressed by the overall high quality of the entries we have received. The imagination, energy and creativity which has gone into each young writer's entry made choosing the best poems a challenging and often difficult but ultimately hugely rewarding task - the general high standard of the work submitted amply vindicating this opportunity to bring their poetry to a larger appreciative audience.

We sincerely hope you are pleased with our final selection and that you will enjoy *Once Upon A Rhyme Cheshire* for many years to come.

Contents

Tessa Neale (10)   25
Catherine Broome (8)   26
Otto Emmerich (8)   27
Heidi Neale (8)   28

Dane Bank CP School

Aaron Brookes (8)   28
Macauley Pedder (7)   29
Roger Nguyen (7)   29
Charley Robson (8)   29
Grace Keane (7)   30
Jennifer Swainson (7)   30
Amy Regan (9)   31
Kyle Lunt (7)   31
Connor Sutton (7)   31
Joseph Costin (10)   32
Konrad Clough (8)   32
Charlotte Downs (9)   33
Jade Owens (9)   33
Aimee Jenner (8)   34
Matthew Walker (8)   34
Andrew Cook (9)   35
Saffron Silver (11)   35
Luke Pirie (8)   36
Joseph Nuttall (8)   36
Laura Marshall (10)   36
Paige Doherty (10)   37
Abdul Sahid (11)   37
Ryan Kelly (11)   37
Sam Goodwin (10)   38
Hannah Milnthorp (10)   38
Nicola Fisher (10)   38
Jamie Hardman (9)   39
Matt McPherson (9)   39
Shamim Khatun (9)   39
Jason Hankinson (10)   40
Jessica Cooper (7)   40
Jenny Cossey (10)   40
Jessica Large (8)   41
Farrah Goodwin (8)   41
Alysha Reilly (10)   42

Jack Corcoran (10)	60
Nina Loncar (10)	61
Eleanor Hughes (10)	61
Emily Chappell (9)	62
George Caddick (9)	62
Alexander Manning (10)	63

Offley Junior School

Lauren Edwards (9)	63
Will Porter (10)	64
Sophie Phillips (9)	64
Emma Holmes (11)	65
Natalie Williams (11)	65
Morgan Smedley (9)	66
Yasmin Tredell (11)	66
Ally Pursglove (9)	67
Lee Taylor (10)	67
Zena Tredell (9)	68
Emily Hudson (9)	68
Robin Bonar-Law (9)	69
Zoë Hardman (9)	69
Alex O'Neill (9)	70
Danielle Stanway (7)	70
Siannie Pryor (10)	71
Isobel Porter (7)	71
Philip Chadwick (10)	71
Zachary Williams (9)	72
Holly Stephenson (7)	72
Isobel Williams (11)	72
Abigail Coyne (10)	73
Lauren Jeffs (9)	73
Eleanor Doubleday (7)	74
Stephanie Farrar (10)	75
Harriet Stubbs (9)	75
Luke Olpin (10)	76

Pinfold CP School

Rebecca Craddock (9) & Mia Hodgkinson (10)	76
Sam Shepperd (10)	77
Joe Knott (10)	77
Jordan Rowswell (9)	77

Chloe Ogden (10)   77
Kay Brotherton (9)   78
Christopher King (9)   78
Jessica Melles (9)   78
Ryan Whittaker (9)   79
Lauren Hawthorne-Brooks (10)   79

Queens Road Primary School
Megan Johnstone (7)   79
Christopher Durbin (8)   80
Sophie Pullen (8)   80
Nadia Belkacemi (9)   81
Jack Bates (7)   81
Bethany Cashmore-Tranter (8)   82
Georgia Hendrick (8)   82
Joshua Ridgway (8)   83
Natalia Jain (7)   83
Dylan Macartney (8)   83
Nikita Jain (11)   84
Reece Marsden (7)   84
Emine Fraser (8)   85
Jade MaCartney (7)   85
Jade Elliot   86
Lucy Dixon (8)   86
Emily Prince (8)   86
Rachel McLoughlin (8)   87
Alex Forrest (7)   87
Lottie Shepherd   87
Alexandra Heatley (11)   88
Corina Ositelu (7)   88
Emma Fidler (10)   89
Callum Farrand (9)   89
Oliver Bethell (11)   90
Meesha Anwar (9)   90
Rachel Gunn (9)   91
Gemma Carrigher (10)   91
Jack Willett (9)   92
Francesca-Mae Warren (11)   92
James Ramsden (10)   92
Nicholas Bryan (10)   93
Sophie E Butterworth (10)   93

Sophie Jane Butterworth (11)	94
Samantha Bradley (10)	94
Chloe Igoe (11)	95
Jamie Menzies (10)	95

Ravenbank Community Primary School

Georgia Spencer (10)	96
Nicola Jones (10)	96
Rebecca Carroll (11)	97
Max McDonough (11)	97
Stephanie Linnell (10)	98
Phoebe Hamill (11)	98
Christopher Dawson (10)	99
Harriet Dawson (11)	99
Sam Whiteford (10)	100
Jack Woodward (10)	100
Michael Freeman (10)	101
Sarah Affi (10)	101
James Robinson (10)	102
James Atkinson (10)	102
Helen Rex (10)	103
James Foreman (10)	103
Esme Shattock (10)	104
Harriet Morley (10)	104
Peter Minaeian (11)	104
Karina Schelze (10)	105
Laura Smyllie (11)	106
Christian Birchall (10)	106
Mark Sarkar (10)	107

St Ambrose RC Primary School, Adswood

Joshua Davenport (11)	107
Aislinn Walsh (10)	108
Emma Downs (11)	109
Jackie Battersby (11)	110
Darcie Walsh (10)	110
Chlöe Farrow (10)	111
Darcie Walsh (10)	111
Jessica Yates (10)	112
Hannah Lawler (11)	112

St Bede's RC Primary School, Weaverham

Jacob Foster (9)	113
Georgia Hamnett (9)	114
Emily Pointon (9)	114
Andrew Brown (9)	115
Rebecca Whittaker (9)	115
Jonathan Stitch (9)	116
Molly Burrows (9)	116
William O'Toole (9)	117
Alice Jones (9)	117
Jodie Hughes (9)	118
Charlotte Owens (10)	119
Patrick Geoghegan Shaw (9)	119
Aiden McTasney (9)	120
Georgina Shepherd (9)	120
Felicity Geary (9)	121
Megan Pointon (9)	121
Niamh Smith (9)	122
Christopher McNabb (9)	123
Alice Pointon (9)	124

The Firs School

Matthew Burgess (9)	124
Emily Cook (10)	125
Isobel Sherlock (9)	125
Georgia Cook (9)	126
Olivia Archer-Jones (10)	126
Jennifer Drummond (10)	127
Cassie Austin-Kaye (11)	127
Alice Holden (10)	128
Georgina Holmes (11)	128
Maria Loizou (10)	129
Camilla Bird (10)	129
Sarah Willetts (9)	130
Charlotte Graves (10)	130
Kitty Green (10)	131
Zoe Duckworth (10)	131
Amy O'Brien (10)	132
Katie Greenwood (11)	132
Catharine Verity (11)	133
Thomas Kerr (10)	133

The Weaver Primary School

Katie Rowland (8)   151
Emma Wilmer (8)   151
Kathryn Spiers-Pritchard (9)   152
Lois Wylie (8)   152
Samuel Narici (9)   153
Oliver Tollafield (8)   153
Tom Young (11)   154

Tilston Parochial CE Primary School
Christopher Duffy (9)   154
Rachel Jane Ewins (9)   155
Emma Ewins (11)   155
Alexandra Eleri Hunter (10)   155
Abby Cooper (11)   156
Jack Adie (9)   156
Adam Flanagan (9)   156
Hannah Rachel Littler (10)   157

Tyntesfield Primary School
Lottie Brown (7)   157

Underwood West Junior School
Nicola Taylor (10)   158
Kelly Chedotal (10)   158
Kelsey Jade Shaw (9)   158
Chantelle Butters (11)   159
Lauren Kaye (11)   159
Robert Wardle (9)   160
Paris Waller (9)   160
Alice Brown (10)   161
Anthony Steven Tweats (11)   161
Emily Sproston (9)   162
Alicia Hollinshead (9)   162
Sam Crookham (11)   162
Ryan Jones (9)   163
Samantha Mason (10)   163
Dean Larvin (10)   163
Ashley Turner (10)   164
Ryan Allen (10)   164
Andrew Gorringe (8)   165

Lisa-Marie Beran (9)	165
Sean Aaron Reilly (8)	165
Danielle O'Connor (8)	166
Katie Hollinshead (8)	166
Shannon Dowling (9)	166
James Woolrich (9)	167
Sean Arnold (11)	167
Kyle Wright (8)	167
Adam Hopley (10)	168
Callan Holland (8)	168
Amber Titterton (10)	168
Kyle Scane (11)	169
Lauren Astbury (8)	169
Nikki Cooke (8)	169
Jason Purcell (10)	170
Jessica Smith (9)	170
Kyle John Beech (10)	170
Jack Roberts (9)	171
Aaron Beresford (11)	171
Abigail Lyn Murray (8)	171

Victoria Road Primary School

Charlotte Nuttall (11)	172
Stephen Lawes	172
Sarah Rockliffe (11)	172
Brogan Ashley (10)	173
Danielle Nickson (10)	173
Holly Davies (10)	173
Michael Fryer (11)	174
Elly Campbell (10)	174
Natalie Clutton (9)	174
Matthew Sanders (10)	175
Adam Rockliffe (9)	175
Daisy Collins (9)	175
Amy Groome (9)	176
Kate Allman (9)	176
Jack Kirkham (9)	176
Rebecca Lyon (9)	177
Ashley Smith (10)	177
Stefan-Kevin Gallimore (10)	177
Nikita McNulty (10)	178

Abbie-Leigh Jones (10)	178
Thomas Turner (10)	178
David Alexander (11)	179
Nathan Evans (10)	179
Melissa Ann Hough (10)	179
Lee Davies (9)	180
Connor Watson (9)	180
Zack McDonald (10)	180
Jonathan Bate (10)	181
Stevie Stewart (9)	181
Luke Roberts (10)	181
Fayad Uddin Choudhry (10)	182
Daniel Ward (11)	182
Steven Mulholland (10)	182
Elizabeth Parr (9)	183
Jenna McLean (9)	183
Sam Evans (10)	183
Kirsty Purvis (10)	184
Adam Malam (10)	184
Emma McCarthy (9)	184
Simon Morrall (10)	185
Tiffany Littlemore (10)	185
Ben Butler (10)	185
Naomi Groome (11)	186
Ryan Histon (10)	186
Christopher Birchall (11)	187
Daniel Quinton (9)	187
Rachel Purvis (11)	188
Kimberley Hughes (9)	188
Victoria Smith (9)	189
Andrew Donald (9)	189

Well Green Primary School

Richard Underwood (9)	189
Ellie Armitage (8)	190
Penny Silverwood (9)	191
Alice Gill (8)	191
Alexandra Norbury (9)	192
Savannah Walker-Ellis (9)	192
William Bundey (8)	193
Jack Surplus (8)	193

Lydia Smith (9)	194
Olivia Papworth (9)	194
Rebecca Jones (8)	195
Jack Lenihan-Smith (9)	195

Winnington Park Primary School

Becky Niblett (10)	195
Madeleine Bullen (11)	196
Rohini Solanki (9)	196
Rachel Bousfield (9)	197
Kathryn Hooker (8)	197
Matthew Payne (11)	198
Robyn Conway (10)	198
Vivien Ravenscroft (10)	199
Sam Davey (11)	199
Sarah Barclay (11)	200
Emma Brown (10)	200
Jessica Hewitt (9)	201
Ella Finn (11)	201
Sophie King (11)	202
Aiden Barrett (10)	203
Sher-Ling Tang (11)	204
Tom Hewitt (11)	205
Abby Hardie (11)	205
Zak Anderson (11)	206
Annabel Johnson (10)	206
Siobhan Allmark (11)	207
Rachael Ann Fryer (11)	207
Amy Woakes (11)	207
Daniel East (10)	208
Lauren Randles (11)	208

The Poems

Elephant

Ears like long sparkling fire swerving in each direction.
Legs like big tree trunks squashing everything in sight.
Feet like big killing machines stomping on the ground.
Eyes like small black eyes spotting everything in sight.
Trunk like a big swerving serpent looking for food.
Tusks like big teeth of the woolly mammoth.
Body like a big sumo.
Grey like the colour of its mother.

Joe Robinson (8)
Arlies Primary School

Elephants

Elephant ears are like butterfly wings.
Elephant legs are like the trunk of an oak tree.
Elephant feet are like round circles of light.
Elephant eyes are like tiny, dark pebbles.
Elephant trunks are as long as a snake.
Elephant tusks are like strong, white paper.
Elephant bodies are as big as a rushing river.

Katie-Leanne Cliffe-Hares (8)
Arlies Primary School

Elephant

An elephant is a very large animal.
Ears like a fluttering butterfly.
Legs like a squashy orange.
Feet so big they can make the earth quake.
Eyes like very small tiny mice.
Trunk like a slithering snake that slides around.
Tusks like wonderful diggers used to pick things up.
Body as grey as a big cloud ready to start raining.
An elephant is a large animal.

Laura Ogden (8)
Arlies Primary School

I'm Talking Loud!

I'm talking loud!
I'm talking shrill!
I'm talking thundering,
Rowdy,
Full volume,
I'm talking noisy
Ear-splitting,
Deafening,
Booming!
I'm talking full blast,
Piercing,
I'm talking loud!

Shannon Carty & Jack Edwards (7)
Arlies Primary School

Elephant

Giant but calm it will always defend its family.
Ears like rabbits' floppy ears.
Legs like lots of people standing straight.
Feet as flat as a pancake and as strong as a brick.
Eyes like gleaming, shiny marbles.
Trunk as slithery as a snake in long grass.
Tusks as sharp as razor-sharp claws.
Body as big as a truck.
Grey like metal shining in the night.
Elephant, giant but calm,
It will always defend its family.

Ben Alexander (7)
Arlies Primary School

I'm Talking Mean!

I'm talking mean!
I'm talking foul!
I'm talking disgusting,
Nasty,
Terrible!
I'm talking wicked,
Horrible,
Appalled,
Aghast!
I'm talking dreadful,
Disagreeable,
I'm talking mean!

Amy Robinson & Christopher Hudspith (7)
Arlies Primary School

Untitled

I have seen many bloods in the things I have done,
I have fought many battles and many I have won.
I have seen men suffer and fall to the ground,
My blade has been swung around and around.

My blade has been cleaned to wipe the blood,
My owner once died and I was dropped in the mud.
I have seen many people die in a war,
There are some truly gruesome things
I wish I never saw.

Christopher Brearley (9)
Arlies Primary School

I'm Talking Raw

I'm talking raw!
I'm talking cool!
I'm talking unheated,
I'm talking icy,
Wintry!
I'm talking bitter,
Crispy, frosty,
Nippy!
I'm talking chilly, evening,
I'm talking raw.

Andrew Bellavia & Jack Royle (8)
Arlies Primary School

My Dog Sally

I have a black and white dog
Whose name is Sally,
And she is sometimes fierce
And she is sometimes pally,
But whether she is black,
Or whether she is white,
There's a patch on her tail
That makes her mine.

She has a long tongue,
That is long and pink
And it hangs down low,
When she wants to think,
She seems to think lots
When it is rather hot,
She is really a good dog,
She plays with the dog called Ally,
That is my dog Sally.

Laura Smith (10)
Bollington Cross CE Primary School

The Snake Shalott River

(Based on 'The Lady of Shalott' by Alfred Lord Tennyson)

Shooting through the trees
Going as fast as the breeze
Each have different keys
They are almost as rapid as the seas
The snake river of Shalott

Curling, curving as bows
Nobody knows how far the river flows
Further, further the river goes
The snake river of Shalott

The crackling laughs of the witch
Her voice is very high pitch
Her face is a lonely stitch
Doing spells that make her filthy rich
The curse of the witch

Conquering the lonely curse
Acting like an old sly nurse
The curse of the witch.

Elliott Simpson (10)
Bollington Cross CE Primary School

The Lady Of Shalott

(Based on 'The Lady of Shalott' by Alfred Lord Tennyson)

Shalott river snake slithers and swishes
Into the river of Camelot splashing and hissing
On the floor his colours were lashing
On the river to Camelot

Fortress of Camelot looking
Down from up above
Almost touching the sky
Rushing and gushing, sun shining
As the breeze blows them away
Looking over Camelot.

Nicole Hiles (10)
Bollington Cross CE Primary School

The Lady Of Shalott And The Snake

(Based on 'The Lady of Shalott' by Alfred Lord Tennyson)

The snake spirit river
Is a snake that slithers
In the day it slithers
And in the night that shivers
It swishes side to side
Snake sticks its tongue out
Like a fast bird.

As the Lady of Shalott watches
It makes her feel happy
The river down Camelot
The river down Camelot

The snake spirit river
Slithers across the stones
At night and day it says hello
To the Lady of Shalott

She is just dreaming
Having no fun
I wish I was outside
She didn't know what to do
River down to Camelot.

Fay Connor (8)
Bollington Cross CE Primary School

The Lady Of Shalott

(Based on 'The Lady of Shalott' by Alfred Lord Tennyson)

The lilies blow in the beautiful lands,
Their petals fly like dancing hands,
She slaves all day with serious demands,
Her hands full with different sands,
The fortress Camelot.

Her life is lonely, the mirrors all she had,
But just thinking about Lancelot makes her glad,
If the spell awaits her I might add,
No more Lady of Shalott.

To the coffin she shall go,
A silver garment perched down low,
In the boat there laid a dead woman, 'Oh no!'
Dead at the hands of her evil witch foe,
The cry of Camelot.

In the coffin she did lie,
For once she saw the deep blue sky
With her last ounce of strength, she let out a cry,
Sir Lancelot caught her in the corner of his eye
The Lady of Shalott.

Mary Thorp (9)
Bollington Cross CE Primary School

The Lady Of Shalott

(Based on 'The Lady of Shalott' by Alfred Lord Tennyson)

Then all the people stood bright,
Feeling very unhappy,
Oh what they said a pity sight,
They all cheered with gleams around,
Going around sad at night off,
Going around sad at night off.

Then all the people stood bright,
Feeling very unhappy,
Oh what they said a pity sight,
They all cheered with gleams around,
There she lies in boat afloat,
Floating everywhere happily,
There she floats happily,
There she floats happily.

In a coffin there she lay,
There soon she heard the music play,
People round the grave that day,
Did weep tears, had little to say,
Buried down in Camelot.

Rosie Margerson (9)
Bollington Cross CE Primary School

The Lady Of Shalott

(Based on 'The Lady of Shalott' by Alfred Lord Tennyson)

Shalott's snake river sways down the rocks,
In the scaly water.
To stay awake is all she begs.
Floating down to Camelot.
There she laid it seemed so long,
Something came out, it was a tongue.
If he dies it will go all wrong,
The man that lifted her was strong,
As sang her last song.

Jessica Kenyon (9)
Bollington Cross CE Primary School

The Lady Of Shalott

(Based on 'The Lady of Shalott' by Alfred Lord Tennyson)

In the water a coffin afloat,
She hopped in and used it as a boat,
In her song a wonderful note,
Getting wet her blood-red coat.
The rivers of Camelot.
The big white planet's light of the moon,
Washing along the sky-blue lagoon,
Knowing her damp dark death, was coming soon,
Her life ends in Shalott!

A coffin lay in the windowpane,
Then she heard her lover's name,
She got in her coffin; it was such a shame,
But then her lover came
And saved her from her death,
It was 12 o'clock noon,
She thought she was going to die soon,
Her last song was a wonderful tune,
Thinking it was her last breath!

Daniel Bates (10)
Bollington Cross CE Primary School

The Lady Of Shalott

(Based on 'The Lady of Shalott' by Alfred Lord Tennyson)

Floating down the blue lagoon
Humming, singing a merry tune
Stars are shining from above
Her voice was a coo of a dove
The Lady of Shalott

There she lies in a wooden boat
Managing to keep afloat
Her time of death is coming slow
Why, why, why does she have to go?
The spirit of Shalott.

Nikki Woolley (9)
Bollington Cross CE Primary School

The Lady Of Shalott

(Based on 'The Lady of Shalott' by Alfred Lord Tennyson)

In the coffin there she lay,
Then soon she heard the music play,
People round the grave that day,
Did weep tears had little to say,
Buried down in Camelot.
Her red coat was still not dry,
She had one tear as she began to cry,
As she left she decided to die,
The Lady of Shalott.

Then she slept and woke in fear,
Then above her she saw a spear,
She was a skeleton as she appeared,
She banged the top, with a tear,
As she was in Camelot.
She scared nearly everyone,
Then she saw her lover as she was upon.
The Lady of Shalott.

Shannon Clark (9)
Bollington Cross CE Primary School

The Lady Of Shalott

(Based on 'The Lady of Shalott' by Alfred Lord Tennyson)

In the bushes and the leaves
She lived with nature in the trees.
She flies with all the fluffy bees
And carefully listens to the breeze
Now daring to look on Camelot.
She can look down on the small sea.
'Now I'm dead, I'm fully free
And shall be forever me,'
Whispered the fairy of Shalott.

Sebastian Searle, Nick Chadwick, Scott Foulds (10),
Mathew Ainsworth, Megan Bennett (9) & Jake Bennison (8)
Bollington Cross CE Primary School

The Snake And The Eagle

A slithery newborn snake,
Once explored on her own,
She had a scaly, wet-like back,
She was abandoned and left alone.

At dusk snake saw her
Shape on the soil
'Hey, people look at me,
I'm lengthy, high and loyal.'

Snake's shadow was vast,
She wailed, 'No eagle scares I!'
An eagle then swooped
And ate snake with, snake in a cry.

Deceit by her lengthy shape
That lay long on the floor base,
Snake's self-respect meant that she
Was no longer on the Earth face.

Ella Hilton (10)
Bollington Cross CE Primary School

The Lady Of Shalott

Based on 'The Lady of Shalott' by Alfred Lord Tennyson)

In the coffin there she lay,
Soon she heard the music play,
People round the grave that day,
Did weep tears had little to say,
Buried down in Camelot,
Buried down in Camelot.

Woken by the noise of digging,
She soon found out she was living,
The Lady of Shalott saw the tower pinging,
She could hear the bird singing,
The breeze was noisy, and tingling,
The breeze was noisy, and tingling.

Alice Bennison (8)
Bollington Cross CE Primary School

Working In The Mines

It was a dark, gloomy night
Drop, drop, drop.
I almost had a fright
Drop, drop, drop.
It was as black as coal
Drop, drop, drop.
I fell down a hole
Drop, drop, drop.

It was as cold as ice
Drip, drip, drip.
My master wasn't being very nice
Drip, drip, drip.
I found a nice little girl
Drip, drip, drip.
The girl's name was Annie
Who had a little curl
Drip, drip, drip.

The mine workers working
Drip, drop, drip.
Children lurking
Drip, drop, drip.
Coal in the fire
Drip, drop, drip.
I tripped over a wire
Drip, drop, drip.

Katie Bennett (8)
Bollington Cross CE Primary School

The Lady Of Shalott

(Based on 'The Lady of Shalott' by Alfred Lord Tennyson)

Years before this present day,
A curse was conjured, upon her it lay,
With an evil devil they all say,
'She never left that curse at bay.
But left beloved Camelot'
Unaware of the power at first,
She ran away to escape the curse.
'I am sorrowful, but I deserve,'
Said the Lady of Shalott!

Years after her life was lost,
She never again was double crossed,
But lived in happiness, head truly tossed,
Gliding over trees truly mossed,
In forest Camelot.
'I am dead,' she said, with glee,
Staring over the old oak tree,
She was happy, happy to see,
That at last she appeared to be free,
Free was the Lady of Shalott.

Megan Skelhorn (10)
Bollington Cross CE Primary School

General Wocky

(Based on 'Jabberwocky' by Lewis Carroll)

'Twas midday, and the Bathing Thorntails
Did swim and roll in the stream:
All shaky were the red mushrooms' tails -
And the General was a dream.

Beware the General my fox!
He's evil that mass, the claws that are brass!
Beware the spirit Andros and box
The ferocious tyrannosaurus nass!

He took his ancient staff in hand:
Long time the eager foe he pursued -
So rested he by the fire plant tree,
And stood awhile in thought.

And as in deepish thought he stood,
The General with eyes of flame,
Came charging through the bulgy wood
And cried as he came!

Hit, slash! Hit, slash! The General and he
The ancient staff went snicker, smack!
He left him dead and with his head
He went galumphing back.

'And hast thou slain the General?
Come to my place my beamish boy
O fabulous day! Tallooh! Tallay!'
He chortled in his joy.

'Twas midday, and the Bathing Thorntails
Did swim and roll in the stream:
All shaky were the red mushrooms' tails -
And the General was a dream.

Samuel Clark (11)
Bollington Cross CE Primary School

Children At Work

Working in mines all the time
Clackety-clack! Clack!
The people who run this must be a crime
No! No! No!
I have never had any fun
And I will never see the sun.
Hope! Hope! Hope!
I don't have any friends
When will this ever end?
Cry! Cry! Cry!
I hurt myself under the machines
Trying to get them clean.
Ow! Ow! Ow!
I am always lifting crates
And no help from my mates.
Alone! Alone! Alone!
Bosses whipping
I'm always tripping.
Pain! Pain! Pain!
I hear some dripping
And they start whipping.
Help! Help! Help!
I start crying
While my family is dying.
Oh no! Oh no! Oh no!
I haven't got a home
Because I'm all alone.
Home! Home! Home!
I never want to see the sun rise
On another day of this torture.

Olivia Benson (8)
Bollington Cross CE Primary School

Jabberwocky

(Based on 'Jabberwocky' by Lewis Carroll)

'Twas twilight, and the dodgy DJ,
Did twist and boogie in the night,
All funky were the break-dances
And the minstrels outplayed.

Beware the teacher, my disco diva,
The moves that kill, the legs that twirl,
Beware the dum dum dances and halt
The break-dancing boys.

He took his dancing right over the top,
Long time the terrible teacher foe sought he,
So rested he by the DJ decks
And stood a while in thought.

And in feverish thought he froze,
The teacher with eyes of flame
Came boogieing through the sweaty crowd
And whirled as she came.

Hip, hop, hip, hop and twist and twirl,
His grooves and moves went tippa tap,
He left it standing and with her glasses
He came spinning back.

And hast thou out-danced the teacher?
Come to my arms my disco diva, hooray, hooray
Oh fantastic day
He boogied in his joy.

'Twas twilight, and the dodgy DJ
Did twist and boogie in the night
All funky were the break-dances
And the minstrels outplayed.

Kevin Broome (11)
Bollington Cross CE Primary School

Jabberdancery

(Based on 'Jabberwocky' by Lewis Carroll)

'Twas 3am and the dodgy DJ
Did tremble and dance in the hall
All drunk were the dads
And the sequin girls outsing.

Beware the teenager my dancing friend
The breath that smells, the fights, the fights that are born
Beware the mum - mum guards
And leave the break-dance boys

He took his vorpal dancing in pride
Long time the teenager he sought
So rested he by the biscuit bin
And sat a while in thought

And as in wonder he stood
The teenager with breath of smoke
Came charging through the crowded disco,
And danced as if to provoke

One, two, one, two and through and through
His vorpal dancing was challenged at last
He threw him out and without doubt
He went dancing past

Has thou out-danced the teenager?
Come to me my dancing boy
Oh fabulous day!
Hooray, hooray, he jived in his joy

'Twas 3am and the dodgy DJ
Did tremble in the morning
All drunk were the dads
And the sequin girls outsing.

Jordan Wilson (11)
Bollington Cross CE Primary School

Jabberwocky

(Based on 'Jabberwocky' by Lewis Carroll)

It was twilight and the slimy toads
Did watch and wriggle in the wave,
All mummies were the bossy ones
And more rats overgrow.

Beware the jabberwock my son
The jaws that bite, the claws that catch
Beware the jubjub bird and shun
The furious toadsnatcher.

He took his deadly sword in hand:
Long time the frightening foe he sought,
So rested he by the tumtum tree
And stood awhile in thought.

And as in confusing thought he stood,
The jabberwock, with eyes of flame,
Came whooshing through the tangly wood
And bellowed as it came, 'Arrgghh!'

One, two! One, two! And through and through
The deadly blade went snicker-snack
He left it dead and with its head
He went galumphing back.

'And you have slain the jabberwock
Come to my arms my joyful boy
Oh fabulous day! Hooray! Hooray!'
He chortled in his joy!

It was twilight and the slimy toads
Did watch and wriggle in the wave,
All mummies were the bossy ones
And more rats overgrow!

Jamie Baskerville (11)
Bollington Cross CE Primary School

Jabbermockery

(Based on 'Jabberwocky' by Lewis Carroll)

'Twas Friday and the glittery girls
Did prance and preen in the disco.
All mimsy was DJ Groves
And Mr Jones stayed low.

Beware of the dance teacher my friend!
Her moves, that snarl, her thoughts that crawl
Beware the action bird and shun
The shining disco ball!

She took her glass of wine in hand
Long time she danced until she fell
So rested she by the school wall
And sat with her friend Mel.

And as in disco mood she sat
The dancing teacher with arms of power
Came pushing through the hall doors
And twisted for an hour.

She turned real fast as she went past
Her dancing feet went clicker-clack
She left them stunned and with their hands
They went clapping back.

'And has thou got the glamour Emily?
Come to the bench beamed lazy boys
Oh, frabjous day, hooray hooray,'
They chortled in their joy.

'Twas Friday and the glittery girls
Did prance and preen in the disco
All mimsy was DJ Groves
And Mr Jones stayed low!

Emma Connelly (10)
Bollington Cross CE Primary School

Jabberwocky

(Based on 'Jabberwocky' by Lewis Carroll)

'Twas brillyart and the slibery tuves
Did grudy and dimgle in the labe
All limsy were the boruguves,
And the gome ragths outglabe.

Beware the jabberwock, my son!
The jaws that bite, the claws that catch!
Beware the jubub bird, and shun
The frumdious bansnatch!

He took his dangerous sword in hand:
Long time the manome foe he sought
So rested he by the tumum tree
And stood awhile in thought.

And, as in unffish thought he stood,
The jabberwock, with eyes of flame,
Came whiffing through the tigey wood
And burbled as it came!

One, two! One, two! And through and through
The dangerous blade went pnicker-pnack!
He left it dead, and with his head
He went galphingd back.

'And hast thou slain the jabberwock?
Come to my arms, my beamish boy!
O fabjous day carlooh! Caray!'
He chortled in his joy.

'Twas brillyart and the slibery tuves
Did grudy and gimgle in the labe
All limsy were the boruguves
And the gome ragths outglabe.

Sara-Louise Bowring (10)
Bollington Cross CE Primary School

Jabberwocky

(Based on 'Jabberwocky' by Lewis Carroll)

It was shining and slithery toads,
Did shine and spread in waves,
All were happy the smelly groves,
And the home of them is brave!

Beware the jabberwock, my friend,
The jaws that bite, the claws that catch,
Beware the jubjub bird,
The furry thing attacks and snatch!

He took his sword in hand,
Long time since his last fight,
So he rested by the tumtum tree
And stood while he thought.

And stood and stood, and thought and thought,
The jabberwock, with eyes of flame
Came struggling through the green wood,
And sniggered as he came.

Two, three, two three, let's go, let's go,
The metal blade went snicker-snack!
He left it dead, and with his head
He went galloping back.

'And have you killed the jabberwock?
Come cuddle me, my great boy!
Oh what a day, callooh! Callay!'
He shouted in joy.

It was shining on slithery toads,
Did shine and spread in waves,
All were happy the smelly groves,
And the home of them is brave!

Stacey Fenwick (11)
Bollington Cross CE Primary School

Jabbermockery

(Based on 'Jabberwocky' by Lewis Carroll)

It was twilight and the slithery toads
Did gyrate and gobble in the wave
All bumpy were the ancient roads
    And the mome raths outgrabe.

Beware the jabberwock my boy
The jaws that bite, the claws that catch!
Beware the jubjub bird and shun
    The furious bandersnatch!

He took his sharp sword in hand:
Long time no see his foe he sought
So rested he by the autumn tree,
    And stood awhile in thought.

And as in the movie he thought,
The jabberwock, with eyes of flame,
Came whistling through the ugly wood,
    And burbled as it came!

One, two! One, two! And through and through
The dangerous blade went snicker-snack!
He left it dead, and with its head
    He went galloping back.

'And did you kill the jabberwock?
Come to my arms my friend!
O frabjous day! Callooh! Callay!'
    He chortled in his joy.

It was twilight and slithery toads
Did gyrate and gobble in the wave
All bumpy were the ancient roads
    And the mome raths outgrabe.

Vicki Rigby (11)
Bollington Cross CE Primary School

Jabbermockery

(Based on 'Jabberwocky' by Lewis Carroll)

'Twas 7 o'clock and the disco divas
Danced gyre and gimble in the gym
All mimsy was DJ Borogrove
And everyone was grim.

Beware the dodgy DJ my friend
His tunes that snarl, his decks that bite
Beware the harmony bird and shun
The evil disco light.

She took her ideal CD in hand
Long time she danced till she perspired -
So rested she by the gym wall
And stood awhile so tired

And in joyless thought she stood
The dodgy DJ with eyes of flame
Came mixing through the cloakroom doors
And sung as he came

She thought real fast as he went past
Her dancing feet went snicker-snap!
She left him stunned and with his tunes
She went galumphing back.

'And has thou got the tunes, Jackie?
Come to our decks,' beamed the idle boys.
'Oh triumphant day, hooray, hooray!'
They chortled in their joy.

'Twas 7 o'clock and the disco divas
Danced gyre and gimble in the gym
All mimsy was DJ Borogrove
And everyone was grim.

Rosy Emmerich (10)
Bollington Cross CE Primary School

Jabbersocky

(Based on 'Jabberwocky' by Lewis Carroll)

'Twas 2-2 and the midfielders
Did hop and flop on the pitch.
All shy was our keeper
And our coach fell in a ditch.

'Beware their goalkeeper, my lad
His dives that block, his legs which crop!
Beware the evil ref and Parry
The giant leg fouler!'

He took his muddy ball in feet,
Long time since he last touched it,
So dribbled the ball down the pitch
And ran for the target.

And as he reached the open goal
The keeper, with eyes of flame
Stared menacingly at the ball
And exercised again.

One, two! One, two! And through and through!
And the ball flew in the net!
He left him stunned and with the ball
He went galumphing back down to the rest.

'And hast thou scored a goal?
Come to my arms my favourite boy!
Oh, frabjous day! Callooh! Callay!'
He cheered in his joy!

'Twas 3-2 and the midfielders
Did hop and flop on the pitch
All shy was our keeper
And our coach fell in a ditch.

Aaron Holtappel (11)
Bollington Cross CE Primary School

Jabberwocky

(Based on 'Jabberwocky' by Lewis Carroll)

'Twas brilliant, and the slimer tuves
Did tyre and pimble in the wade
All bimsy were the boronuves
And the tome raths outgrate.

Beware the jabberwock, my son!
The jaw that bites, the claws that catch!
Beware the gubgub bird, and sun
The frumious sandasnatch!'

He took his frilling sword in hand
Long time the manxome foe he sought
So rested he by the tumtum tree
And stood awhile in thought.

And, as in ouffish thought he stood
The jabberwocky with eyes of flame
Came whitling through the tulgy wood
And burbeld as it came!

One, two! One, two! And through and through.
The vorbal blade went ticker tack
He left it dead, and with his head
He went galloping back.

'And has thou slain the jabberwock?
Come to my arms my beamish boy!
Oh frabjous day, callooh, callay!'
He chortled in his joy.

'Twas brilliant and the slimer tuves
Did gyre and pimble in the wade
All bimsy were the boronuves
And the tome raths outgrate.

Tessa Neale (10)
Bollington Cross CE Primary School

In The Mines

It was dark
Crash! Bang!
Except a little spark
Crash! Bang!
It was full of dirt
Crash! Bang!
Suddenly someone got hurt
Crash! Bang!
It was cold
Crash! Bang!
It was 60 years old
Crash! Bang!
I will never see the fun
Crash! Bang!
I will never see the sun
Crash! Bang!

I will never see the sunset
Crash! Bang!
It's getting wet
Crash! Bang!
It was getting colder like ice
Crash! Bang!
I was surrounded by mice
Crash! Bang!
It was getting dirty like mud
Crash! Bang!
It was like a big flood
Crash! Bang!
It was getting darker like coal on a fire
Crash! Bang!
I was surrounded by wire
Crash! Bang!
I was alone
Crash! Bang!

Catherine Broome (8)
Bollington Cross CE Primary School

The Working Mill

In a dim room, children labourering,
Working day and night
Grind, grind the flour
No sleep
No food
No water
Only *grind, grind* the flour.
Old rags, unhappy and sick
Grind, grind the flour
Children working day and night.

Bosses banging, beating, whipping
Grind, grind the flour.
Crash! Bang!
Oh no, the machine fell on Burty!
I hope he is alright
'Get back to work,' said the boss.
No going to sleep
What is sleep? I ask myself.
Grind, grind the flour
Children working day and night.

Clank, clank
Thank goodness Burty is alright
Grind, grind the flour.
Too tired to work.
Grind, grind the flour.
Children working day and night.

Otto Emmerich (8)
Bollington Cross CE Primary School

The Mines

I'm hardworking and my name is Holly
Clang! Bang! Boom!
I try to be happy but I'm never, never jolly
Clang! Bang! Boom!

I work in the mines
Clang! Bang! Boom!
I'm always on time
Clang! Bang! Boom!

I cry and I cry
Clang! Bang! Boom!
I'm very, very shy
Clang! Bang! Boom!

And when I'm all alone
Clang! Bang! Boom!
I will see the sun
Clang! Bang! Boom!

Heidi Neale (8)
Bollington Cross CE Primary School

A Snowy Night

One snowy night I heard a noise,
I suddenly woke up,
So I went downstairs,
To see what it was.
My mum was excited and I was as well,
My mum let me go out for two minutes
And then I had to go back to bed.
I couldn't wait until the morning,
So then I fell asleep
And my mum carried me to bed.

Aaron Brookes (8)
Dane Bank CP School

Snow

One snowy day I went to school
And saw my friend make a snowman
And then the bell rang.
The other children were crying
Because they didn't have a go.
They were crying in class,
But when it was playtime
The kids wanted to play with the snow
But it had melted in the sun.

Macauley Pedder (7)
Dane Bank CP School

Snow

The snow had fallen,
I could see snow as white as clouds,
I could hear children laughing,
I could feel snow as cold as ice,
I could smell tasty meat,
I could taste snow, very cold.

Roger Nguyen (7)
Dane Bank CP School

On A Snowy Night

It was a snowy night
And I was the only one out.
I started to play.
It was dead crunchy and icy.
Then I found a really icy bit,
But as soon as I was going to play with it
My mum called me in.

Charley Robson (8)
Dane Bank CP School

The Snow

When I woke up one morning I saw the snow,
There was one boy playing in it and that was Joe,
I asked my mum could I play out,
But then she started to shout,
So I got dressed and asked her again,
But my little sister was driving her insane,
I had my breakfast and asked my dad,
But his car was driving him mad,
So I decided to go up to him,
But he had to go to the gym,
So I asked my auntie Dawn,
But my new cousin had just been born,
So I asked my uncle Mark,
But his dog started to bark,
So I asked my cousin Annie,
But she was talking to her boyfriend Danny,
So I asked my grandad,
But he was very sad,
So I asked my mum once and for all
And I eventually got to play with a snowball.

Grace Keane (7)
Dane Bank CP School

Snow

There was snow on the playground,
One snowy morning I woke up yawning.
When I got dressed my bed was a mess,
I went outside, the snow looked like a white blanket.
I tasted a cold snowflake, it was like a lolly.
Icicles dripped from cars, the road was slippery.
There was snow on the trees,
But then the snow was melting.

Jennifer Swainson (7)
Dane Bank CP School

On A Snowy School Day

Snow is as white as Father Christmas' beard,
Joe was playing in the snow,
I hear children shouting and screaming,
People throwing snowballs at each other,
After a few days the snow melts,
The touch of the snow was very cold,
The taste of snow is just the same as water,
The sight of snow is as white as can be.

Amy Regan (9)
Dane Bank CP School

Snow

One snowy day I went to school
And saw a lot of snow
Some more children came to school
And I had a snowball fight with my friends
I got in trouble
So that was the end of my playtime.

Kyle Lunt (7)
Dane Bank CP School

The Snow

I was dreaming of some snow
When I woke I saw snow
I went to play outside
But my dad started to shout
The next day I went to the shop
To buy a sledge
I slid to the edge of the road
And I hurt myself.

Connor Sutton (7)
Dane Bank CP School

Snow Emotions

As I drew the curtains I saw it . . .
Crisp white snow as far as the eye could see.
A brilliant sparkle, a lovely sight, a white blanket.

I saw someone walking with his head hanging down,
His footsteps trailing behind him.
A lonely fellow, a shuffling walker, an unhappy chap.

As I looked further, I saw some scruffy lads
Having a snowball fight. It looked like a fun game,
A whale of a time, a dodging war.

Oh how I wished I could join them,
Oh how it made my heart sad,
Oh how I hated my wheelchair.

Joseph Costin (10)
Dane Bank CP School

Snow Day

When I came downstairs to get a drink
I looked out the window at night,
I thought I was dreaming
And my mum let me out to play in the snow.
It looked like a crinkled page
And my friends came out and had a snowball fight.
Then we went to bed.

In the morning the snow was so cold
And we had some ice on the road.
I rushed to school and all the snow hurt my eyes.
It was so bright me and Callum started a snowball fight.
At dinnertime I ate as fast as I could to see Year 5s wall
And I could hear children screaming
And then it was time to go home,
But I could play in the snow at home.

Konrad Clough (8)
Dane Bank CP School

Snow

I love snow,
It's crunchy on my feet,
It's cold in my hands,
It makes me shiver,
I make snowballs and throw them at Jessica,
I get covered in snow by Mr Curden,
I throw snow at him,
He loses his glasses in the snow,
I made a snowman at my house,
My cat, Smoky, didn't like the snow,
A snowball hit me in the back,
Becky skidded across the ice,
A snowflake went in my mouth,
It was cold and wet,
I love snow, it's great fun.

Charlotte Downs (9)
Dane Bank CP School

Snow At School

Snow is like ice but softer,
It is white as a flock of sheep.
Snow is more fun than your favourite and best toy
And you just trust me
And believe it or not it is.

Snow is fabulous and snow is funny,
Snow is great and also fuzzy,
Throw a snowball at the teacher,
And if you hit him or her
You will probably get it thrown back at you.

As the snow falls to the ground
It drifts through the air with a silent sound,
It covers the tree, it covers the town,
It sparkles in the moonlight then shimmers till dawn.

Jade Owens (9)
Dane Bank CP School

A Snow Poem

In the night I woke up,
My dog was barking at the snow,
It looked like bits of clouds falling,
The morning came, I went outside,
The snow was crunching on my shoes,
The snow was still falling, it fell in my mouth,
It felt very cold like an ice cube.

On the way to school, it was noisy,
At school I got hit with a snowball,
I tried to make a snowman
But it fell down.
I had a snowball fight,
Mr Cruden lost his glasses in the snow,
After that it was time to go home.

Aimee Jenner (8)
Dane Bank CP School

Snow

Snow is fine
Snow is white
Snow is joyful
Snow is light
Snow is ice
Snow is as white as a piece of paper
Snow is cold
Snow is plain
Snow is horrible in the rain
I like the texture of snow
I like a snowball fight with my friends
And I love snow.

Matthew Walker (8)
Dane Bank CP School

Slipping

Opening the doors
Seeing the snow.
People slipping,
Children shouting.
Traffic beeping,
Stuck in the snow.
Boys playing in the snow
Girls crying,
Hit in the face.

Boys skiing,
Drinks freezing,
Rivers iced.
When will the snow melt?

Andrew Cook (9)
Dane Bank CP School

Snow

'Hooray, it's snowing,' everyone shouted,
The school field was covered in snow,
White glistening, gleaming, shining snow,
People were throwing snowballs this way and that,
People were charging up and down the field,
Throwing snowballs at each other.
You can taste the water in your mouth,
As people throw enormous snowballs at you,
You wipe the freezing cold water off your face,
Your gloves are soaking wet,
You can't feel your fingers or toes,
I go and tell the teacher but after all,
It's only snow.

Saffron Silver (11)
Dane Bank CP School

Snow

Snow is fine, snow is white
Snow is joyful
And I wish it would come every night.
When I play in the snow
It feels like I'm on a cloud,
When snow turns to ice I slip a little.
I hear children crying and having fun
And when they're happy I'm happy too..

Luke Pirie (8)
Dane Bank CP School

One Snowy Day

Snow is a cloud in the sky.
Snow is like a piece of crumpled paper.
Snow is as cold as an ice cube.
Snow is white as a white beard.
Snow is as shiny as the white school sink.

I felt really excited to play snowball fights
And it was fun to build a snow wall.

Joseph Nuttall (8)
Dane Bank CP School

Snow

Hear the crunching of feet in the snow,
See the snow as white as sheep,
Glistening like a silver diamond.

Taste the snow as cold as ice,
It is as soft as cotton wool,
Making drivers go round the bend,
Because of its bright, dazzling whiteness.

Laura Marshall (10)
Dane Bank CP School

Snow Poem

The jolly children play happily outside,
With the soft snow that feels like cotton wool
And looks like a sheet of white crumpled paper,
That glistens softly under soft blue sky,
You can smell the cold, fresh air
And all you can hear is children shouting happy things,
Until they go back into school.

Paige Doherty (10)
Dane Bank CP School

Snow

A gleaming white, white duvet,
Along the green grass.
The relaxing earth
Under the mass.

The coldness of snow,
Is as cold as ice.
People having fun,
As snow falls it looks like rice.

Abdul Sahid (11)
Dane Bank CP School

Snow

The snow was deep and all so crisp
It's as white as a flock of sheep
The children were playing and having fun
'Take this!' 'Take that!' 'Coming through!' they shouted.

The snow felt like cotton wool
Wow, hot icy, how cold, how crunchy
When it falls it looks wonderful
The trees as white as never before
All on a winter's morning.

Ryan Kelly (11)
Dane Bank CP School

A Winter's Day

Walking past my garden wall,
I saw my neighbour,
His son and I went to play in the snow,
On a sleigh dashing through a winter day,
Wondering what to do the next day,
Opening my curtain now,
How the snow has gone
And I'm going back to school,
That is dull.

Sam Goodwin (10)
Dane Bank CP School

Snow Night

At night you lie in your bed
and the snow starts to fall.
It starts off slow and gets faster.
I look out of my windows,
snowballs are flying past your windows.
Kids crying in the street.
I just can't wait to get out.
I put my coat on with my hat,
scarf and gloves.
I went outside as fast as I could.

Hannah Milnthorp (10)
Dane Bank CP School

Snow

I smell the fresh, cold snow
I taste the wetness in my mouth
I see the older and younger children having a snowball fight.
I hear people crunching their feet in the crunchy snow.
I feel the freezing wet, soggy snow in my hands
And that is what it's like for me when it snows.

Nicola Fisher (10)
Dane Bank CP School

Snow

When I woke up at night I saw the sparkling snow,
It was as white as an ice cream, it crunched like a biscuit,
It is like freedom playing with Joe, my friend,
I hear people playing in the wonderful snow,
It is like a cloud in the sky,
It was a World War III,
I made a wall with all my friends,
But it got wrecked by Year 6 and Year 5!

Jamie Hardman (9)
Dane Bank CP School

Snow

Snow is as white as crumpled paper,
You can hear people slipping
And I hear them shouting, 'They're attacking!'
I throw a snowball at Jamie,
Then covered him in snow.
People were attacking so we made a wall,
It was as white as a cloud in the sky,
It was as white as lumpy paint,
Thank you God for snow.

Matt McPherson (9)
Dane Bank CP School

Snowy Night

The snow is as white as a white board
Snow twinkles, snow glows
I hear children shouting, 'Snow! Snow!'
Snow is cold, snow is white
I like to see it very bright
I love the snow
I love to play for 3 hours with my friends
We all went home very late.

Shamim Khatun (9)
Dane Bank CP School

Snowy Night

I see the snow one dazzling night,
All so fluffy and so bright,
I charge outside with my hat and gloves,
As I approached the snow that looks like doves,
It sounds like I've stood on a crisp,
As my sister and her boyfriend just kissed,
What a great snowy night.

Jason Hankinson (10)
Dane Bank CP School

The Snow In The Playground

One snowy day, I went to school,
With my mum and my friends Nicole and Charley.
When I got in the playground
It was dead icy and skiddy.
When it was playtime everyone was playing
On the ice with their friends.
But me, Nicole and Charley weren't,
We were playing Charlie's Angels in the snow.

Jessica Cooper (7)
Dane Bank CP School

A Snowy Night

On a really snowy day,
I walked down the street.
The snow looked like some silver glitter
And some white clouds in the sky.
Like some tin foil wrapped up,
In some apple pie.
It looked like some feathers from a bird.
It sounded like a crunching noise.
It crumbled down under my feet
And it melted in my hands.

Jenny Cossey (10)
Dane Bank CP School

I Love Snow

I love snow, especially when it's everywhere,
I love to throw snowballs at my friends and family,
They throw them back at me,
It's really fun, they enjoy it too.

When it snows it suddenly becomes the best time of year for me,
Classes 5 and 6 made a big snow wall,
Classes 3 and 4 also tried to make one too but we couldn't,
We didn't really mind though, we still did well.

I tried making a snowman but I gave up,
I wish that snow was here every second, every minute,
In fact all the time.

Jessica Large (8)
Dane Bank CP School

Snow

Snow glows in the winter weather,
You hear children play,
The snow is like living on a cloud,
When it glows it's like the sun,
Sometimes you feel warm in the snow
Because you are covered up,
Running round and playing,
You have joyful fun with snow,
It's sometimes low,
Then you think what a lovely world
God has given us.

Farrah Goodwin (8)
Dane Bank CP School

Snowy Day

On a cold winter's day,
As I was opening the door,
I stopped in amazement,
There in front of me was white, crispy snow,
I walked out of the house,
Into the deep, soft snow
And then I could hear my sister running towards me,
In her hand was a massive snowball.
All morning she was chasing me
Up and down the street.
In the end I gave up
And she threw it right at me,
What a horrible big sister.

Alysha Reilly (10)
Dane Bank CP School

The Snowy Day

The snowy morning when I woke up
My mum's car was white as a cloud
And my grandad had to drive very slow,
To take me to school.
When I got to school I could hear
The children laughing
And my friend Charley
Had built a gigantic snowman.
My teacher Miss Bishop came to school late,
So Jackie had to look after thirty children.

Megan Kelly (8)
Dane Bank CP School

White

White is a plain of icy snow,
It's a letter just come through the post,
It's a lonely town,
It's an empty heart,
It's a frozen pond,
It's someone who dragged you into nowhere,
A stream of rushing tears,
It's a sheet of dull paper.

Hannah Booth (9)
Havannah CP School

Limericks

There once was a lady from Crewe
Who painted her face bright blue
She looked in the mirror
Then had big shiver
And the next day she had the flu.

Holly Yates (8)
Havannah CP School

Black Is . . .

Like a pebble falling from the sky into a raging stream of water.
Like a piercing voice towering over you.
A stream of tears pouring down my face.
It feels like being alone with the air hunting you down.
Like a dungeon of rats creeping in and out of their lairs.
A graveyard with a frightening galleon darting after you.
An animal limping through the middle of the night.

Cade Spence (10)
Havannah CP School

What Am I?

Fluffy, fat and evil
Sometimes fast, sometimes slow
And likes meat and honey
And I don't like the snow
So that's my riddle that is all.
Can you guess what I am called?

Laura Barlow (9)
Havannah CP School

Turquoise

It's a tropical sea
It's energy and emotion
It's a fresh glass of water
It's a lonely tear
A shark slicing through the sea
It's in a water fight.

Adam Howarth (10)
Havannah CP School

Green Is . . .

A hard voice turning inside out
It's the smell of a new pen
It rushes to an empty lane
It's a lovely light feeling
A dirty tower singing above the dark blue sky
It's a race that never stops
A reflection that always says . . .
Goodbye.

Christopher Welch (10)
Havannah CP School

Green . . .

Is the smell of newly mown grass,
It's a sick day when you can't play,
It's a lime-tingling taste in your mouth,
It's sports day when you win a race,
It's being disagreeable.

Edward Grisedale (10)
Havannah CP School

Brown Is . . .

Brown is a musty, muffled voice
It's a vicious murder
It's a milky, chocolate river
It's a dirty trick
In a scrumptious chocolate cake
Sounds like a flute playing a lazy tune
In a lonely town.

Gabrielle Booth (9)
Havannah CP School

A Day At The Theatre

I went to the theatre
The theatre of dreams,
Where the stage is green
And the players are mean,
The crowd chanted and cheered
As the ball broke the net.
It's the best place I've been yet.

Tom Greenfield (10)
Navigation Primary School

Memories

I remember, I remember the house which I was born
The garden in which I pricked myself simply on a thorn
The kiss goodnight, tucked in all tight until the morning will come
Then I'd get up just in time to get a cuddle from Mum.

I remember, I remember my first day at school
The day in which my teacher said, 'Follow every rule'
I met some friends and it was fine until I had to go
When I got home to tell my mum all she said was, 'Oh!'

I remember, I remember the time I had a job
I came home to a load of mess since I was a slob
Eventually I got married and found the love of my life
And when we cut the wedding cake we also kept the knife

I remember, I remember when I passed away
And now I get fresh flowers every single day
I look over my family to make sure they're OK
And when they are in trouble I'll be here to stay.

Jenna Wilks (11)
Navigation Primary School

On A Say Day

The way you got buried,
I could not watch.
The sand getting put on your coffin,
Made me wish that it didn't happen.
The parties we had for your birthday,
Bought all the memories back,
Of playing on the swings,
That reminds me of eating chicken wings.
You brought all the fun,
But never stuff.
We're lost outside,
But please come inside.

Kelebogile Nteta (9)
Navigation Primary School

If

If you're lonely and have no friends,
Don't just hide, join in,
If you believe, you will do well
All through your life,
Never doubt yourself, or anybody else
And they won't doubt you.

If you want to be treated well,
Then treat others how you wish to be treated,
If you always try your best,
There is an even chance of getting it right,
If you care, others will care,
Do this and you will be welcomed.

If you win others will lose,
Don't boast or you will be hated,
And if everybody is your friend
You will be everybody's friend.

Emma Cusick (10)
Navigation Primary School

In The Haunted House

In the haunted house it's scary and creepy,
In the haunted house it's wet and leaky,
In the haunted house it's dark and sleepy,
In the haunted house it's spooky and sneaky.

In the haunted house I'm on my own,
In the haunted house I'm in a zone,
In the haunted house I need a phone,
In the haunted house I should have known.

In the haunted house I see a light,
In the haunted house I hear a noise,
In the haunted house I hear a mate,
In the haunted house I escape.

Nicole Boone (9)
Navigation Primary School

Where Do All The Teachers Go?

Do they mark our homework?
Are they living on Mars?
Do they ever brush their hair
And do they drive space cars?

Do they ever do any sport?
Running, swimming and football?
Do they ever go to the gym
And do star jumps in the hall?

Do they ever eat a lot?
Chocolate, ice cream and more?
Do they ever play PC games
And do they get a high score?

Do they ever do anything fun
Like watching the TV?
Do they like all the soaps?
Are you sure they're like you and me?

I'll follow one back home today
I'll find out what they do
Then I'll put it in a poem
That they can read to you.

Christopher Carruthers (11)
Navigation Primary School

Candy Tree

I love candy, candy is sweet, candy is sour,
Chocolate is milky, banana is power.

I like trees, green trees and red ones, even pink,
Tree add candy, it makes a candy tree.

The candy tree is a wishing tree
For granting wishes for everyone!

Sarah Morris (8)
Navigation Primary School

On The Pop, Thud, Crash

On the pop, thud, crash
The mice turn to ash
And Mr Busby went snap
While Mr Longworth goes flap
On the crash, thud, pop
Mrs Westlake goes sly
Mr McLuckie goes fry
Mrs Glue goes stick
And Mrs Patterson goes thick

On the pop, thud, crash
Mrs Walsh goes ping
Mrs Woodword doesn't know a thing
Mrs Jones goes whizz
Mrs Milton goes fizz
On the crash, thud, pop
Mrs Whittaker goes boom
Mrs Carcary goes crack
And Mr Hodgson goes to have a snack.

Christopher Carr (11)
Navigation Primary School

Tropical Sea

In the morning when the golden sun and the tropical sea
Glides across the golden shore,
When the morning dies and it's midday
When the children tromp along the shore
Tromp, tromp, tromp,
While you're trying to get to sleep
It's not fair.
When it turns dark night
And the stars twinkle with the moonlight
And it blinds you because of the light.

Connor Toward (9)
Navigation Primary School

Rain

Sat inside keeping warm,
Drip-drop, drip-drop
You see the rain splashing on your window,
Pitter-patter, pitter-patter,
Listen to the rain dripping on the ground,
Splish, splash, splish, splash,
Drip-drop, drip-drop,
Pitter-patter, pitter-patter,
Splish, splosh, splish, splosh,
Splash, splash, splish, splish,
Dripping off your garage roof,
Hear it splash on the ground,
Slowly getting heavier,
Noise getting louder,
Splish, splish, splosh!

Bethany Dibnah (10)
Navigation Primary School

Snake Began

He took the blade of a knife
He took the end of a pitchfork
To make his tongue

He drank the poisonous water
He took the blood out of humans
To make his venom

He took the skin of a fish
He took the shiny shell of a turtle
To make his skin

He took the movement of a worm
He took the squirm of a maggot
And made his slither

And snake was made.

Alex Palin (9)
Navigation Primary School

Animals

Animals in jungles
Animals in forests
Animals in farms
They're everywhere

Animals who roar
Animals who swim
Animals who fly
They're all different

Animals with stripes
Animals with spots
Animals with fins
They're all beautiful

Animals are scary
Animals are lazy
Animals are friendly
They're all unique.

Carolyn Jalaly (9)
Navigation Primary School

The World Under The Sea

Small sea caves dingy and dark,
Where the water is all a blur,
Where the hazy water taps and strokes
Where the bright sea plants tangle and squirm;
Where the many fish swim rapidly past,
Keeping together in a shoal, swimming, swimming;
Feel the damp sand below your feet.
Watch it float in the sea pouring up and around,
Swim with the flow of the moving water,
Let it take you farther and farther, deeper and deeper . . .

Jessica Lister (11)
Navigation Primary School

Where Do All The Teachers Go?

Where do all the teachers go,
When the school is out?
Do they go straight to bed,
Or round the roundabout?

Where did they learn all the stuff they tell us?
Was it because of school?
Did they do their maths and things
And then head to the swimming pool?

At what age did they finish school?
Was it as bad for them?
Was for the usual sixteen years,
Going again and again and again?

Did they ever spel rongly?
Did they ever use bad grammar?
Was it so harsh for them?
Did they only learn one manner?

I'll follow one back home today,
I'll find out what they do,
Then I'll put it in a poem
That they can read to you.

Liam Douglas (11)
Navigation Primary School

Season Haikus

Winter season
Blisteringly cold
Ice cubes tickling in my mouth
Icicles dropping.

Autumn season
Golden leaves floating
Slowly swooping quickly fall
Then they stay right down.

Joseph MacCann (9)
Navigation Primary School

Why?

Why do people fight?
Why do people hurt?
Why, why, why?

Why do we pollute the air
With our poisonous gases?
Why do we murder
With our guns?
Why, why, why?
Why don't we get along,
Why do we bully?
Why can't there be peace,
All around the world?
Why, why, why?

All these questions
And no answers?
Why, why, Why?

Amy-Louise Robertson (11)
Navigation Primary School

Dolphin Began

She began
She took water from the sea
She took smooth gel to make it shine
And made her skin

She took the sky
She took the black sky
And made her eyes

She took summer echoes
She took a cry of a baby
And made her voice

And the dolphin was made.

Fay Hand (9)
Navigation Primary School

What If . . .

There's something I'd really like to know,
Is it yellow, orange or blue?
Is it big, small, high or low
Or maybe something new?

What if the trees were made of bricks
And all walls made of wood?
All candies were like sticks
And all different types of mud?

What if people didn't talk
And were happy when looking sad?
Their favourite dishes were white chalk
And they loved to get mad?

What if dinosaurs were here
With yellow and pink spots?
Children were made to stay near
Lots and lots and lots?

What if the sky was very green
And teachers were not nice?
The schools were not very clean,
And fishes could eat rice?

I'll find out one summer's day,
And spread it out a lot.
I'll tell you if fish eat hay,
And when the North Pole gets hot.

Yasmin Lawal (10)
Navigation Primary School

If

If you can control your anger
Even when it is strong.
If you cannot lash out
When people are calling you names.
If you can be patient
And never get frustrated with someone.

If you can tell the truth
Confess when you know you have done wrong.
If you can keep a promise
Forever and ever.
If you can make a friend
And are friends for years.

If you never judge people
By their colour or appearance
If you can smile even when you are sad
And everyone will smile too.
If you can help a person
Even if you don't get on.

If you are miserable
Don't moan or whine.
If you respect everyone and everything
Then everyone will do the same for you.
If you can do all these things
Then you truly deserve to be on Earth!

Joe Bodden-Glennon (11)
Navigation Primary School

A Poem About Me

If I were an animal I would be a monkey,
hairy, clumsy and small.

If I were a bird I would be a dove,
patient, calm and quiet.

If I were a piece of furniture I would be a three-piece suite,
cold, comfy and big.

If I were a fruit I would be an apple,
crunchy, juicy and ripe.

If I were a musical instrument I would be a drum,
loud, round and big.

If I were a vehicle I would be a Ferrari,
loud, flash and quick.

But I like being me
because I can play football.

Thomas Crawford (11)
Navigation Primary School

Where Did All The Teachers Go?

Do they eat with cutlery?
Do they ever clean their plate?
Do they have table manners?
Are they ever late?

Do they go to town with mates?
Do they ever get drunk?
Do they drink lots of beer?
And come home like a skunk!

Do they ever exercise?
Do they go to a gym?
When we have music homework
Do they practise hymns?

Thomas Andrews (10)
Navigation Primary School

Where Do All The Teachers Go?

Where do all the teachers go
After it goes dark?
Do they sleep upside down
Or have a dog that can bark?

Do teachers have feelings?
If so about who?
Do they live in a hole
Or ever need the loo?

Do they have a soul
Or can they fly?
Do they drink people's blood
And if so why?

At night do they sleep
Or can they teleport?
Can they run around
Or even play sport?

I'll follow one home tonight
To find out what they do
And put it in a poem
For them to read to you!

Jack Kirvin (11)
Navigation Primary School

In A Place Under The Sea

In a place under the sea
Where the fish float and flee
The dolphins dive and play
And the hagfish sleep all day

In a place under the waves
Where octopuses lie in caves
The limpets stick to rocks
And the peacock worms peer out in locks.

Bethany Hunt (10)
Navigation Primary School

An Earthquake

In an earthquake pots and pans,
Clatter, clatter, *bang!*
Cupboards open things fall out,
With a *clang!*

Lights smash,
Tables bash,
The clock falls down with a crash.

Pencils slide,
Rulers glide,
Run away and hide.

Things boom,
Things zoom,
All around the room.

Earthquake's over, not a sound,
Stuff has fallen all around.

Rebecca Coombs (9)
Navigation Primary School

The Underworld

When all goes dark and the moonlight shimmers,
And all the decaying skulls start to glimmer,
When the head of the pirates all dead and rotten,
Start to come alive from head to bottom,
First all the arms and legs start to move
And then the fingers move into groove.

The ship starts to rock and creak as it does,
There is no other sound, not even a buzz,
The odd fish would swim by,
Being caught by a skeleton fisherman and eaten in a pie.

Lewis McBride (10)
Navigation Primary School

The Kidnapper

As the gusts of wind howl in the night,
There comes a shadow, creeping down the long dark road . . .
All in pitch-black clothes, underneath you can see a bright pair
Of silvery eyes leading the way.

As the clock strikes midnight,
The footsteps start to go quicker
As the shadow paces down the road.
His light footsteps aren't to be heard.
Suddenly the shadow comes to a halt.

The shadow looks left to right,
Then frantically climbs up a house,
His gloves gripping anything he sees,
Then does his second stop at a top window . . .

His black-gloved hand reaches through,
And as quick as a flash, grabs a child,
Waking it from its dream.
Then quickly takes off his glove
And covers the child's mouth with his sweaty hand.
He rushes back down the house
With the poor child in his grasp
And runs off into the darkness,
That poor child in his grasp is *me* . . .

Isabel Gillet (10)
Navigation Primary School

Winter Haiku

Blue ice-cold winter
Children having snowball fights
Ice cubes in a drink.

Marcus Wilkinson (9)
Navigation Primary School

If I . . .

If I were an animal I would be a dolphin
Friendly, helpful and careful

If I were a bird I would be a dove
Peaceful, kind and sensible

If I were a piece of furniture I would be a leopard-skin couch
Wild, posh and furry

If you could eat me I would be a lamb
Cute, harmless and nice

If I were a musical instrument I would be a saxophone
Jazzy, shiny and hard

If I were a vehicle I would be a limo
Long, stylish and sexy

But I like being me because I'm good overall.

Brett Davidson (11)
Navigation Primary School

What Are . . . Bugs?

Bugs are parasites of the forest,
That poison your garden and leave it to die.

Bugs are slaves with never-ending work,
Carrying loads back and forth with no break.

Bugs are escaped criminals running from the feet of officers
Never stopping - avoiding everyone, in one place they'll never stay.

Bugs are cars with legs, running on air
That after a short time break down - permanently.

Jack Corcoran (10)
Navigation Primary School

Clouds

Clouds look like Santa's beard,
All chopped off into the sky.
Clouds are like sheep,
Except sheep don't fly!

Clouds look like mashed potato,
Or a poodle, or cotton wool,
Even froth on some beer,
Some clouds are even like skulls!

Dark clouds on a rainy day
Are no fun,
Now they look like black sheep,
And they've got me feeling glum.

Black clouds are big spiders dancing,
They're shiny, deep tar,
So bad on this day
Now that's what clouds are!

Nina Loncar (10)
Navigation Primary School

Run Hurdles

What do we need?
Speed
Let's go fast to win the race
So what do we need?
A steady pace
I can see that last high hurdle
So what do we need?
A big high jump
Let's finish the race and see the scores,
So run our paws, and look, I've come *first!*

Eleanor Hughes (10)
Navigation Primary School

Rain, Pitter-Patter

Pitter-patter, pitter-patter,
Drip-drop, drip-drop.
Clitter, clatter, clitter, clatter,
Hip, hop, hip, hop.

Hear the rain on the ground,
Pitter-patter, pitter-patter.
Whirling round and round,
Pitter-patter, pitter-patter.

Pitter-patter, pitter-patter,
What are we going to do now?
Pitter-patter, pitter-patter,
Tell me how.

Pitter-patter, clish, closh,
Splish, splosh, hiss, hoss.

Emily Chappell (9)
Navigation Primary School

Trees

Trees are humans standing and staring,
Trees are ghosts lurking in the dark.

Trees are beer froth rising and growing higher to look over everyone,
Trees are babies growing from an egg to an adult,
Trees are thousands of eyes at others everywhere.

Trees are statues standing still for hundreds of years,
Trees are humans with a fan when the leaves blow,
Trees are whales whining for communication.

Trees are stainless steel never rusting,
Trees are metal and steel never cracking,
Trees are crowds of flowers all stuck together.

George Caddick (9)
Navigation Primary School

Skatepark

Down the ramp, faster and faster,
Picking up speed on the rail
Picking up speed, faster and faster.
Going up one side up the spine
Down the other, gaining speed,
Jumping higher, faster and faster
It's the end of it.

Alexander Manning (10)
Navigation Primary School

I Would Like A . . .

I would like a bell
Made out of a seashell.

I would like a flower
With lots of powers.

I would like a rainbow
Made with snow.

I would like to go to space
And have a race.

I would like a chime
That says a rhyme.

I would like a cat
That says, 'How's that?'

I would like a house
As small as a mouse.

I would like a frog
As big as a dog.

But most of all
I would like to be tall.

Lauren Edwards (9)
Offley Junior School

Hallowe'en

You see the pointed hats
And the flitting flying bats

The cackle of a witch
Lying in a ditch

We see the scary faces
In all the different places

We get sweets
When we ask for trick or treats

We see the ugly frogs
Rotting on the logs

Rapping at the door
There are monsters there for sure

We see the vampires
On the church spires.

Will Porter (10)
Offley Junior School

Happy Thoughts

The most calming laughter on a bright summer's day
And a touch of light breeze in a gentle way
The icy blue sea lapping on the shore
And the cutest smile, smiling every day and more

The happiest family you have ever seen
And the most fantastic place you have ever been
The seasons that you like, especially summer and spring
And your best possession or object or thing

The freezing white snow at wintertime
And the church occasion bells slowly chime
The animals and objects around which I can see
And family, friends and school which is important to me.

Sophie Phillips (9)
Offley Junior School

To Fight For Your Rights

Once upon a rhyme
When life was a crime
You would rush
You would crush
To fight for your rights

> Once upon a rhyme
> To be top of a line
> Would be a quest
> You'd be the best
> To fight for your rights

Once upon a rhyme
To be on time
You'd be a cheetah
You'd beat the beaters
To fight for your rights.

Emma Holmes (11)
Offley Junior School

A Rainbow

A rainbow full of colours
Makes magic in the air,
And people fill with happiness
With a smile as they stare.

At the end of every rainbow
Lies a pot of gold,
A dream that everyone wishes to find
A dream we long to hold.

But then the rainbow starts to fade
The colours disappear,
The magic has gone until next time
And the gold is no longer here!

Natalie Williams (11)
Offley Junior School

Dogs

A big dog,
A small dog,
A large dog
And all different dogs.

A loud dog,
A barking dog,
A quiet dog,
A panting dog
And all different dogs.

A black dog,
A white dog,
A brown dog,
A black and white dog
And all different dogs.

A scary dog,
A fierce dog,
A growling dog
And all different dogs.

Morgan Smedley (9)
Offley Junior School

Rainbow

Red squirrels scampering up a tree,
Yellow ducklings swimming in the sea,
Pink flamingos standing in a lake,
Green grasshoppers acting a fake,
Orange orang-utans eating fruit,
Purple fish in a diving suit,
Blue whales lumber through the ocean,
As if they swim,
In slow motion.

Yasmin Tredell (11)
Offley Junior School

Beano Day!

It's Beano day, the magazine,
But if I don't keep my bedroom clean,
My mother says, 'It is tough luck,
You will not get your Beano book!'

Dennis the Menace and Gnasher too,
Minnie the Minx and Joe Jitsu.
The Bash Street Gang are really bad,
The head and teacher will be mad!

Roger the Dodger is full of tricks,
He'll end up in a terrible fix.
Billy Whiz, as fast as a cheetah,
His mother wishes his bedroom was neater.

Little Plum, the Indian Brave,
Ivy the Terrible likes to rant and rave.
Robbie the Rebel never does as he's told,
He makes out he's tough, brave and bold.

I've reached the last page, this edition was top,
Let's hope that next week's isn't a flop.
I've loved the Beano since I was eight
In my opinion,
The Beano is great!

Ally Pursglove (9)
Offley Junior School

Dream

Dream of a star,
Dream of a face,
Dream of a person,
Dream of a place,
Dream of a city,
Dream of a sea,
Dream of a friend,
I hope it's me!

Lee Taylor (10)
Offley Junior School

Crazy

Is my teacher crazy,
Or is she just plane lazy?
Like my sister too,
Who's jumping on the loo!

Are my relatives crazy,
Or am I going hazy?
Just like my dad,
He has to be *mad!*

Is my hamster crazy,
Or is he bouncing on a daisy?
Just like my fishes
Who are swimming in my best dishes!

Now everyone in this world today is crazy,
So beware when you come out to play!

Zena Tredell (9)
Offley Junior School

My Dog

My dog Skip,
Likes to nip,
The people who come to the front door.

He runs through the house,
Like a cat after a mouse,
We chase him back through
And close the kitchen door,
Where he barks until his throat is sore.

He stops his riot
And goes all quiet,
Ssshhh!

Sound asleep until
The next time a stranger
Speaks.

Emily Hudson (9)
Offley Junior School

Roller Coaster

Twisting, turning,
falling, hurtling,
plummeting to the ground,
going faster than the speed of sound.

Drops, corkscrews,
bends and loops,
Corkscrews spinning round and round,
a loop-the-loop far off the ground.

Slower, slower,
carts go lower,
the carts are waiting to resign
then a shiver ran down my spine.

But off I hopped
the ride had stopped
I was scared but I denied it
and I'll dare my friends to try it!

Robin Bonar-Law (9)
Offley Junior School

Imagine

Imagine a dolphin who could play football.
Imagine a giraffe 12 metres tall.
Imagine the sun was as blue as the sea.
Imagine if we lived in a different galaxy.
Imagine if yellow wasn't a colour.
Imagine if black could be any duller.
Imagine rain was chocolate and sweets.
Imagine whales walking down streets.
Imagine a world just like ours.
Imagine we were all glittering stars.
Just imagine!

Zoë Hardman (9)
Offley Junior School

The Red Rose

The red rose is a plant
It sometimes likes to chant
Its thorns
Are like horns
The leaves that grow on it are as red as blood
They look pretty good
But when snow falls
It curls up into a small brown ball
When winter passes
It emerges out of the ground
Still tired, but still it looks around
And then when winter comes again
The rose does nothing, except the same
A blooming blossom right through its life
Its time will be up, some cold winter's night.

Alex O'Neill (9)
Offley Junior School

Summer Swallow

See the swallow
See the swallow
Gliding through the air

See the swallow
See the swallow
Here, there, everywhere

See the swallow
See the swallow
Flying without a care

How I wish
How I wish
That I could join him there.

Danielle Stanway (7)
Offley Junior School

Silence

Silence like the dead of night
Silence like a really big fight
Silence like the still seas
Silence like the steady breeze
Silence like the children sleeping sleeping
Silence like Ethiopians weeping.

Siannie Pryor (10)
Offley Junior School

Winter

The last autumn leaves
Are blown from the winter trees

Snowflakes cling on branches
Like white blossom

The branches of the trees
Look bare, black and spiky

Snow settles gently on the tree branches
Turning them white.

Isobel Porter (7)
Offley Junior School

A Time

There was a rhyme,
About a boy who played in slime,
He liked it thick, as black as coal,
To find it he would dig a hole,
Like a gas tar baby, he would be,
Goodness gracious, *it's me.*

Philip Chadwick (10)
Offley Junior School

Midnight, Midnight, Midnight

Midnight is when the stars come out
Midnight is where they jog about
Midnight is when the moon says hello
Midnight is where the party starts to grow
Moonlight is made by the sun
Moonlight is fun for everyone
Moonlight, midnight, moonlight.

Zachary Williams (9)
Offley Junior School

Once Upon Enchanted Island!

Far, far away
How far? I cannot say
Lived a pretty little fairy
Whose name was Mary

By day Mary flew
At night she slept in a shoe
Dancing and laughing with her friends
This is where the story ends.

Holly Stephenson (7)
Offley Junior School

The Deep Blue Sea

The sunshine ripples through the sea
Like a plane through the sky.
It's cold and wet but it makes me feel warm inside.
It fills me up with pride to see the glimmer of the sea.
The waves crashing to and fro,
Forwards, backwards, wherever they go.
People playing happy and free,
Girls and boys as young as me.

Isobel Williams (11)
Offley Junior School

Oh Laura

Oh Laura,
Do not leave me,
I plead,
Laura I will miss you,
My friends will too.

Oh Laura,
You are my best friend,
This separation will never mend,
You made me merry,
Your tender face was lovely.

Oh Laura,
My heart is broken,
It cannot be woven,
Is this the end
Of you as my friend?

Abigail Coyne (10)
Offley Junior School

If I . . .

If I was old
I'd be big and bold
If I were small
I'd bounce my ball
If I were smart
I'd be top in art
If I were cool
I'd have a pool
If I were new
I wouldn't know what to do
But because I'm plain
I'm exactly the same.

Lauren Jeffs (9)
Offley Junior School

My Dream!

I dreamed I was a hero,
From out of space,
I dreamed I was a detective,
On a secret case.

I dreamed I was the Queen,
In Buckingham Palace,
I dreamed I worked at McDonald's,
With my friend Alice.

I dreamed I was in a jacuzzi,
Having a great time,
I dreamed I wrote a poem,
Which had to rhyme.

I dreamed I was a pirate,
Sailing the seven seas,
I dreamed I worked with a man,
With knobbly knees.

I dreamed I was making,
A very big snowman,
I dreamed I was in Spain
And I got a suntan.

I dreamed I was a puppy,
Chasing a cat,
I dreamed I was a man,
With a flat hat.

I dreamed I was on The Weakest Link
And I got voted out,
I dreamed I was Ant and Dec,
Toddling about.

I wish I did not have to end,
This lovely poem for you,
So I'll just say goodbye,
Because it's the right thing to do.

Eleanor Doubleday (7)
Offley Junior School

Derby Day

Behind the line at the start of the race,
Number four will set the pace.
'Are you ready?' says number three,
'As ready as we'll ever be!'
There's the pistol, the race is on,
First in line is number one.
Eight overtakes on 'Leggy Devil',
But soon 'Long Shanks' is drawing level.
Over the high log fence they pour,
Long legged 'May-Fly' hits the floor.
All turn back then start again,
Heads bent low against the rain.
Over the wall the hedge and the water,
Next to go down is 'Heaven's Daughter'.
Almost at the end of the track,
Five of them are falling back.
The others tire - just a little,
But 'Tuppeny's' legs grow very brittle.
Drawing near the finish line,
Who breaks the tape . . . ?
It's number nine!

Stephanie Farrar (10)
Offley Junior School

Summer Winds

As the sun burns on my back,
It takes me down the hottest track,
As it drifts through my hair,
It drifts back up into the air.
As we see the flowers that grow,
That seem to blow to and fro,
As we see the bees that go,
It's just like the seasons that teach us to flow.

Harriet Stubbs (9)
Offley Junior School

Myths And Legends

Under the ocean
where the mermaids play
the city of Atlantis
can be found every day.

High in the sky
where the phoenix flies
rising from ashes
it never dies.

Down in the labyrinth
the people lie still
in fear of the Minotaur
who's ready to kill.

Deep within a mountain,
a dragon can be found
fighting off warriors
with a thunderous sound.

These are the stories
from generations old
the myths to the child
repeatedly sold.

But are these just myths
continually told
or real life experiences
from the very old?

Luke Olpin (10)
Offley Junior School

What Is Blue?

Blue is cold water in a swimming pool.
Blue is a dolphin diving out of the sea.
Blue is a classroom chair
Waiting to be sat on.

Rebecca Craddock (9) & Mia Hodgkinson (10)
Pinfold CP School

What Is Red?

An apple is red when it glows on a tree
What is red?
A sports car is red when it speeds through the street
What is red?
A fire is red when it burns.

Sam Shepperd (10)
Pinfold CP School

What Is Snow?

Snow is sugar being sprinkled into a blue bowl.
It is a sweet layer of icing being spread on a rich cake.
It is a white blanket being put onto a sweet just born baby.
It is white chocolate biscuits falling in the night's sky.

Joe Knott (10)
Pinfold CP School

What Is Night?

Night is a big piece of black paper.
Night is ink spilt everywhere.
Night is the sky painted black.
Night is a huge blackboard.

Jordan Rowswell (9)
Pinfold CP School

What Is Blue?

Blue is the eyes of a person,
It is the dolphin swimming
Up and down the sea.
It is a blue sky.

Chloe Ogden (10)
Pinfold CP School

What Is The Sun?

The sun is a drop of sand
mixed with a bit of water,

It is a yellow melon sat on a pale blue plate.

It is a yellow beach ball that
is being played with in the sea.

What is the sun to you?

Kay Brotherton (9)
Pinfold CP School

What Is The Moon?

What is the moon?
The moon is a white fingerprint
On some black paper.
It is some white paint
In a black bin bag.
It is a silver bottle top
On a black step.

Christopher King (9)
Pinfold CP School

What Is Yellow?

It is a sunflower swaying in the wind,
It is a day on the beach,
It is stars in the night sky,
It is sunshine on a summer's day,
It is a lemon in a fruit bowl.

Jessica Melles (9)
Pinfold CP School

What Is Red?

Red is blood on a cut knee
Red is fire in a burning building
Red is Pinfold uniform
Red is a rose in green grass.

Ryan Whittaker (9)
Pinfold CP School

What Are Balloons?

They are fun floating away.
They are paint on blue paper.
They are aliens in a blue spacecraft.
They are planets in orbit.

Lauren Hawthorne-Brooks (10)
Pinfold CP School

Acrostic Poems

A crostic poems are very, very fun
C ome and see my book of poetry
R eally I like a poem that I can play out in the sun
O h really I do like the sun
S o then I can play on my bike
T *ing* my bell rings
I f I fell off, I could hurt myself
C an I have a plaster please Mum?

P oetry is very cool
O h! Can I have a drink?
E verybody has to sit on a stool
M y dad says I am good at poetry
S ome of my friends think I am too and so do I.

Megan Johnstone (7)
Queens Road Primary School

Pokémon

Blazican is very tough
And its skin is very rough

Kyroge is very blue
But it never goes to the loo

Grounden is red
And it never goes to bed

Raquaza is very green
But it doesn't look like a bean

Regirock has rock throw
But it doesn't have a bow

Registeel has metal claw
And it doesn't have a door

Regice has a curse
And it doesn't have a purse.

Christopher Durbin (8)
Queens Road Primary School

Down In The Jungle

Down in the jungle
I met a boy called Jake.
Jake said, 'I can't play now
I'm being strangled by a snake.'

Down in the sea
I met a girl called Jade.
Jade said, 'I can't play now
I am too afraid.'

Sophie Pullen (8)
Queens Road Primary School

My Rabbit

I used to and still do have a rabbit
But I must confess, she has an awful habit.
I say, I do not think
That all rabbits give you a wink.
Oh, and one more thing my rabbit has -
She loves to watch the cartoon Taz!
My rabbit really can do a dance
But really loves to have a glance
At that annoying little baby fox
That's always hiding in a box!
I do not want to end this rhyme
But I think my rabbit's done a crime!
Oh my rabbit and her bad habit.
Hey my rabbit's kind of cute
And her favourite food is mashed up fruit.
I really have to end this rhyme
Cos my rabbit's done a rabbit crime!

Nadia Belkacemi (9)
Queens Road Primary School

Football

F ootball is a game of two sides
O wn goals are dreadful things
O ffside means that there are two men from one team
   and there are two men from the other team that pass forward
   when the men from the other team are together but a gap.
T here are twenty teams in the Premiership, they all have a ground.
B een sent off means you are banned from playing for three matches.
A ll 11 men try to win the match and get three points.
L iverpool are a good football team
L eicester City are rubbish.

Jack Bates (7)
Queens Road Primary School

Number Poem

When I was one
I had just begun

When I was two
I could use the loo

When I was three
I had some tea

When I was four
I broke the door

When I was five
I stood on a beehive

When I was six
I learned some tricks

When I was seven
I ate Heaven

When I was eight
I licked a plate

When I was nine
I made a sign

When I was ten
I cleaned out the pen.

Bethany Cashmore-Tranter (8)
Queens Road Primary School

Sleepovers

Sleepovers are for best friends
Sometimes they can be cool
I love sleepovers
Especially after school.

Georgia Hendrick (8)
Queens Road Primary School

When I Was One

When I was one I ate a bun
When I was two I could use the glue
When I was three I climbed my first tree
When I was four I walked into a door
When I was five I kicked a beehive
When I was six I broke a brick
When I was seven I broke into Heaven
When I was eight I threw my plate.

Joshua Ridgway (8)
Queens Road Primary School

Schools

S chool is . . .
C ool
H ow can you not like it?
O h!
O h it's time for
L unch there's
S omething to munch.

Natalia Jain (7)
Queens Road Primary School

When I Was . . .

When I was one I ate a bun
When I was two I could use glue
When I was three I ate a giant pea
When I was four I kicked down a door
When I was five I ate a beehive
When I was six I learned some tricks
When I was seven my sister was eleven
When I was eight I met my mate.

Dylan Macartney (8)
Queens Road Primary School

Fame

Justin's dances really rock,
Eminem's swearing isn't a shock.
Beyoncé's songs are amazingly cool,
When I sing I sound a fool!

Christina has a deep, low voice,
Everyone likes 50 Cent's lyrics, he doesn't give us a choice!
Black Eyed Peas tell us to 'Shut Up',
And in their concerts you hope to get a close up.

Mis-Teeq sing 'Scandalous'
And all their videos are marvellous.
I dreamt of the Sugababes' 'Hole in the Head',
While I was cuddling up to my ted.

'One Love' is a tune by Blue,
Outside the Arena there is always a queue.
In gorgeous hot Spain,
Ashanti was on the beach singing 'Rain'.

Nikita Jain (11)
Queens Road Primary School

When I Was . . .

When I was one I ate a bun
When I was two I got stuck in the zoo
When I was three I got stuck in a tree
When I was four I trapped my finger in the door
When I was five I ate a beehive
When I was six I swallowed some sticks
When I was seven I made Heaven
When I was eight I ate my mate
When I was nine I drank some wine
When I was ten I made a den.

Reece Marsden (7)
Queens Road Primary School

Number Poem

When I was one
I sucked my thumb

When I was two
I could use the loo.

When I was three
I had my first cup of tea.

When I was four
I cleaned the floor.

When I was five
I learned to drive.

When I was six
I played with matchsticks.

When I was seven
I rescued Mrs Evan.

When I was eight
I broke a plate.

When I was nine
I was just fine.

When I was ten
I made a den.

Emine Fraser (8)
Queens Road Primary School

Down In The Park

Down in the park
I met a boy called Reece.
Reece said, 'I can't play now,
I'm about to watch Grease.'

Jade MaCartney (7)
Queens Road Primary School

Park

P arks are where you play
A ir is great and let's have a great day
R ight here in the sun, let's play with all of them
K ites you fly in the air. See the faces on the people.

Jade Elliot
Queens Road Primary School

Rap!

Dese are my friends . . .
Corina crazy
Lottie lovely
Natalia nice
Connie cool,
Paige positive
And Georgia jazzy.
Well dey are my friends
And de friendship never
Ends.

Lucy Dixon (8)
Queens Road Primary School

Dogs

D ogs are man's best friend
O ur love for them shall never end
G osh bad dogs you can depend
S ometimes drive you round the bend.

Emily Prince (8)
Queens Road Primary School

Under The Sea

Under the sea there are types of whales
Like dolphins, killer whales and other kinds but not water snails
They like to jump and leap out of the water
They play with the whales' daughters.

Rachel McLoughlin (8)
Queens Road Primary School

Rap

When I got into da playground,
De bell was about to ding
Because we had a special visitor,
Dit was the real king.
When I got into da garden,
De wind was blowing hard,
De wind blew so hard,
(I just caught a card),
Dat it blew me out of the yard.

Alex Forrest (7)
Queens Road Primary School

Poem

P oems are cool, don't call me a fool.
O ur family loves to make up poems
E ating while we do our poems
M y mum and dad think poems are cool,
    Poems are not for school.

I love poems, they are really cool!

Lottie Shepherd
Queens Road Primary School

The Swimmer

He walks to the deep end, scared of the water,
Dips in his toe, it's quite cold.
He puts on his goggles, ready for the plunge.
He takes his position, the whistle blows and he dives . . .

Water is all around him,
Full of bubbles.
He seems to be under for hours and hours,
Although it is only a few seconds.
Then he comes up and swims for all he is worth.

He gets to the other side and swims back again.
When he gets back he is tired out,
But he has got what he wants,
The gold medal.

Alexandra Heatley (11)
Queens Road Primary School

Dreams

D reams that are scary will give you a fright
   so much the night won't be good.
R emembering bad dreams you have nightmares
   and you'll call to your mum.
E ating in your dreams might make you feel sick.
   'Mummy stop the night.'
A nd when you've been telling spooky stories all night,
   don't expect you won't get a fright.
M ummy, Mummy, I'm calling you. Oh! Daddy help too.
S limy snakes to bite my eyes out, I'm having a fright in the night.

Corina Ositelu (7)
Queens Road Primary School

The Storm

Dark clouds cover the moon,
The howl of the wolf,
The patter of the rain.

Lightning strikes a tree nearby,
The roar of the fire,
The rain quickens its pace.

The thunder roars over the houses,
The cries of the children,
The rain on the rooftops.

The wind takes down cabins and houses,
Howling and whirling,
The rain is ecstatic.

The fire in the forest dies down,
The moon is revealed,
The rain patters some more . . . and stops.

Emma Fidler (10)
Queens Road Primary School

Fee, Fie, Foe, Fum

Fee, fie, foe, fum I smell the blood of an English mum
Bring her dead or bring her alive
You can even bring her in a beehive.

Fee, fie, foe, fum I smell the blood of an English son
Pull his pants down and his shoes
Then fill them up with lots of tissues.

I think a dad is very sad
Because he hasn't got a wife or son
And he can't say fee, fie, foe, fum.

Callum Farrand (9)
Queens Road Primary School

The Spanish Flea

There was a little Spanish flea,
A record star he thought he'd be,
Like singers,
Like beetles,
Like chipmunks,
He's seen on TV,
There was a little Spanish flea.

There was a little Spanish flea,
A record star he thought he'd be,
Like singers,
Like beetles,
Like chipmunks,
He's seen on TV,
There was a little Spanish flea.

Oliver Bethell (11)
Queens Road Primary School

The Moon

The moon is so bright
It always catches my sight
Half or full it always glitters
On a velvety black night

The moon is so sparkly white
When it's at a certain height
When it hides behind a cloud
And doesn't shine out so proud.

A moonstone to look at
Is always a pretty sight
So beautiful and such a delight
It makes my face beam with light.

Meesha Anwar (9)
Queens Road Primary School

Seasons

Spring is when little lambs grow,
Spring is when flowers bloom,
Spring is a new beginning,
Spring, spring, springtime.

Summer is when the sun comes out,
Summer is when we go on holiday,
Summer is when we go out,
Summer, summer, summertime.

Autumn is when leaves change colour,
Autumn is when leaves fall,
Autumn is when we start to wrap up warm,
Autumn, autumn, autumn time.

Winter is when snowflakes fall,
Winter is when we make snowmen,
Winter is when it's freezing cold,
Winter, winter, wintertime.

Rachel Gunn (9)
Queens Road Primary School

Horses

I like horses they're the best
I like horses they're my friends
I like to ride on them
I like to feed them
I like the way they run
They're so fast
I like the colour of them
I like the way they sound
I love horses so much I want one for myself
I would call mine Megan
Because that's my favourite name.

Gemma Carrigher (10)
Queens Road Primary School

I Love Swimming

I love swimming
Because I think it's really cool
I like diving in one great big pool
I like relaxing in the sauna
I like swimming because it makes me drool.

Jack Willett (9)
Queens Road Primary School

Gymnastics

G is for gold, it looks shiny and nice
Y is for yes, they've got ten twice
M is for men, who are very strong
N is for no, I went wrong
A is for afterwards, when we get a rest
S is for super, you did your best
T is for teamwork, that's what we need
I is for ignoring, the other teams
C is for clever, that's what we are
S is for silver, we got very far!

Francesca-Mae Warren (11)
Queens Road Primary School

The Little Rabbit

There was a little rabbit,
Who had lots of habits
And hopped to me and you.
Then kept on hopping
And couldn't stop dropping.
Down to have a snooze.

James Ramsden (10)
Queens Road Primary School

The Leprechaun Song

There was a little leprechaun,
He had a little friend called John,
They went to the burger place,
He nearly got smacked in the face,
There was a little leprechaun.

There was a little leprechaun,
His little friend has now gone,
Didn't know where he went,
No postcard was even sent,
There was a little leprechaun.

There was a little leprechaun,
His door there came a-knocking on,
He opened it wide
And saw who was outside,
It was his little friend called John.

Nicholas Bryan (10)
Queens Road Primary School

The Winter Storm

The winter storm has started light
In the darkness of the night
Pitter-patter the rain hits the ground
The thunder is sharp and extremely loud.

The wind is whippy and very fast
You can feel the strong wind hurrying past
As the snow starts to fall
It comes down in tiny balls.

The storm is whirling past
As I watched it whirling fast
The storm is getting light
In the darkness of the night.

Sophie E Butterworth (10)
Queens Road Primary School

Famous

How I'd love to be famous
To sing with Blue,
Or Britney Spears and Busted,
Mis-Teeq too.
I'd travel so far on water and sand,
I'd go on 'I'm A Celebrity Get Me Out Of Here!'
I'd swim with the dolphins and walk with the deer.
To dance at clubs all night and day,
Party all night, no one in my way.
I'd talk to the rich and give to the poor,
But all pop stars want is more! More! More!
I wouldn't though, I'd be gentle and kind,
They'd ask for autographs and I wouldn't mind.
I wouldn't be protected, no bodyguard for me,
Lots of fun and I would be free.
I'll be on Pop Idol in five years' time,
So watch out for me and read this rhyme.

Sophie Jane Butterworth (11)
Queens Road Primary School

Cats

I like my cats they're so quiet and soft
And when they're outside they play in the mud
One of them is grey and one of them is black
They pounce on each other because they're two annoying cats

When you stroke them they purr for ages
And when they are at the window and they see a bird
They growl and scratch at the window
But when it's dark they get ready for a sleep
And they curl up in their baskets and fall into bed.

Samantha Bradley (10)
Queens Road Primary School

What Do I Have In My Room?

There were 12 fluffy rabbits leaping up and down
There were 11 cheeky monkeys training to be a clown
There were 10 black bats swooping in my drawers
There were nine naughty cats scratching with their claws
There were eight crawling spiders creeping in my bed
There were seven bumblebees flying past my head
There were six hungry tigers prowling up the sheep
There were five snoring rats falling fast asleep
There were four snorting pigs eating all the food
There were three baby hamsters all in a horrid mood
There were two sparkling fish floating in the tank
There was one grumpy toad chewing on a plant.

Chloe Igoe (11)
Queens Road Primary School

The Toad Who Saved The Day

One day there was a toad
Who lived in the lake where it was cold.

On her broom came a witch
And stole the princess who was rich.

The toad came along to save the day.

He killed the witch and now she's out of the way.

The toad had been under a terrible spell
He turned back into a prince
And everything was well.

Jamie Menzies (10)
Queens Road Primary School

Corrie On The Spot

Coronation Street has a humorous script,
Even when they're eating chips.
In the Kabin lives ranting Rita,
At the bookies cheating Peter.

Poor Kieran dumped at the wedding,
Tracy and the baby that she's dreading.
Roy and Hayley so upset,
Karen and Steve got married for a bet.

Fizz chose Kirk in the end,
Tyrone poor lad driven round the bend.
Nosy Norris makes Emily mad,
Les finding Cilla makes him glad.

Todd and Sarah love each other,
Eileen and Gail the interfering mothers.
I've got to end this poem soon,
Because it's on this afternoon.

Georgia Spencer (10)
Ravenbank Community Primary School

Sunshine

Sunshine, sunshine how you glow,
You shine on the plants and make them grow.
Sunshine, sunshine, oh so bright,
Flooding the world with shimmering light.

Sunshine, sunshine you're a ball of fire,
You're so bright you're hard to admire.
Sunshine, sunshine, you're out in the day,
So me and my sister can go out and play.

Sunshine, sunshine you fade away,
To fall asleep at the end of the day.

Nicola Jones (10)
Ravenbank Community Primary School

Spring, Summer, Autumn, Winter

Spring, summer, autumn, winter which one will it be . . . ?

. . . Spring!
Spring is when we get little lambs
And maybe, the beavers build dams.
Spring is pink and green and yellow
And all colours that are mellow.

. . . Summer!
Summer is hot and sticky,
Which makes my ice cream melt and go icky.
Summer gives me a happy smile,
But my holidays aren't for a while!

. . . Autumn!
Autumn is when leaves drop to the ground
And the wind blows all around.
Autumn is very orange and red,
And all the animals go to bed.

. . . Winter,
Winter is cold and rainy
And I go sledging with my friend Shani.
Winter is fun because it's Christmas time,
And I always leave Santa a bottle of wine!

Rebecca Carroll (11)
Ravenbank Community Primary School

My Day

The flowers blossoming like a golden sunrise
As I see my reflection looking back at me in the slow flowing river.
There's a snow-white butterfly fluttering around my head
As I lie on the velvet-like grass looking up at a golden sky,
Thinking of what beautiful thing will come along next in my day.

Max McDonough (11)
Ravenbank Community Primary School

The Seasons

S pring is here
P retty flowers
R obins singing
I nsects waking
N esting birds
G rowing grass.

S ummer is here
U p comes the sun
M eadows green
M eadows red
E veryone happy
R abbits run.

A utumn once again
U nder the harvest moon at night
T he sight like a golden light
U ntil the sun rose
M ellow pears and brambles
N ew fallen sky.

W inter at last
I cy glitter
N aked trees
T eeth chatter
E arth cold and bitter
R olled in balls of snow.

Stephanie Linnell (10)
Ravenbank Community Primary School

Midge

M y hamster
I ncredibly intelligent
D eliciously daring
G raceful and gentle
E ssential as a pet.

Phoebe Hamill (11)
Ravenbank Community Primary School

The Last Stand

The battle sounds blasted,
Rivers of blood gushing,
Arrows blocking out the sun
Soldiers dropping like flies around me
The surviving soldiers awaiting the next deadly volley
Our archers aiming at the enemy archers but missing
Cavalry Vs cavalry who will win?
Our commander killed, my best friend dead
A cannonball whizzing past my ear killing more men
A stray cavalry man gets shot down
The enemy infantry advance.
Suddenly our cannons shoot taking out loads
Hand to hand fighting begins . . .
More battle horns sound
The enemy's reinforcements have arrived!
Another volley crashes down
More men fall . . .
Our cavalry defeated, the survivors flee
Our archers dead, their archers still shooting
Fog setting in . . .
Our men dying, I ran but I got hit in the back by an arrow.
This is the end . . .

Christopher Dawson (10)
Ravenbank Community Primary School

Penguins

P enguins are my favourite animals
E xtremely excellent at fishing
N ever do they need a net
G racefully gliding through the water
U nique in every way
I cy places are what they like
N aturally nurturing their young
S outh is where they live.

Harriet Dawson (11)
Ravenbank Community Primary School

?

What made the lava flow
Enveloping all friend and foe?

What is like a roaring lion
That ravages everything it sets its eyes on?

What made the bubbling stream
Produce so much gas and steam?

Why did its huge mouth swallow
The mountain path I was to follow?

Why did the fields become
A barren landscape with a blinding sun?

It's awesome, it's deadly, it's overpoweringly huge
But once in a while its magnificence shines through.

(Can you guess what it is?)

Sam Whiteford (10)
Ravenbank Community Primary School

Everything

Every poster paints a picture,
Every picture has a theme.

Every valley has a river,
Every river has a stream.

Every ocean has a creature,
Every creature has its dream.

Every human has a future,
Every future is unseen.

Every poem has a meaning,
This poem's meaning is everything.

Jack Woodward (10)
Ravenbank Community Primary School

I Have A Monster

I have a monster called Fred,
He lives in the garden shed,
His skin is green and his eyes are blue,
But you better be careful,
Or he might eat you!

I have a monster called Bob
And he really needs a job,
His skin is green and his eyes are blue,
But you better be careful,
Or he might eat you!

I have a monster called Mike,
He rides on a motorbike,
His skin is green and his eyes are blue,
But you better be careful,
Or he might eat you!

I have a monster called Ben,
He ate five thousand men,
His skin is green and his eyes are blue,
But you better be careful,
Or he might eat you.

Michael Freeman (10)
Ravenbank Community Primary School

The Bite Of Winter

Winter strips you of all heat like a determined robber;
Slowly but surely.
It will often feel like a long, pointless hike up a steep mountain;
Steeper and steeper and steeper.
Worst of all when the bad boys of winter escape,
They nip your fingers hard till they bleed frozen blood.
When you reach the top of Mount Winter;
Exhausted, tired and weak, look down and feel the warm air
Of the coming spring.

Sarah Affi (10)
Ravenbank Community Primary School

The Bitterness Of Winter

The wind howls,
the cold air whips my face.
As I walk up the path to school,
but it seems that I'm walking up a tall, ragged mountain.
When I see my friends, they are fighting the cold too.
When I'm in the classroom, my body is filled
with warmth, new energy.

When I am outside again,
my fingers begin to tingle,
Dew on the grass,
bleak, frosty, empty silence that fills the playground.
We kick the football in hope we'll get warm,
soon the bell begins to ring,
as we trudge back into the comforting heat.

Lesson times drags on,
quiet, simple, focused.
Tired but happy,
waiting for the end of school,
another trek in the cold bitterness of winter.
The bell rings, again, and another day is over.

James Robinson (10)
Ravenbank Community Primary School

A Proud Blue

I said to my friend, 'Would you like to see
Manchester City play United on my TV?'
He said, 'No, come to mine I've a widescreen TV.'

So off we went to watch them play
I was hoping City would win today
The game was great I have to say.

City won the game 3-2
I heard his next-door neighbour boo
But I just smiled as a proud blue.

James Atkinson (10)
Ravenbank Community Primary School

An Alphabet Of Horrible Habits

A is for Alex who treads on your toes,
B is for Betty who picks her nose.
C is for Carol who teases the cat,
D is for Daniel whose singing is flat.
E is for Emily who slams the door,
F is for Freddy whose jokes are a bore.
G is for Gilbert who gobbles his meals,
H is for Hannah who wears very high heels.
I is for Irin who's sick in the car,
J is for Jill who scoffs jam from the jar.
K is for Kate who keeps candy in bed,
L is for Lesley whose hair is bright red.
M is for Mark who steals from the shops,
N is for Nora who knits baggy tops.
O is for Ollie who pulls wings off flies,
P is for Polly who throws squidgy mud pies.
Q is for Quentin who bellows and bawls,
R is for Rose who graffitis on walls.
S is for Stephen who burps in the baths,
T is for Tom who doodles in class.
U is for Ursula who leaves hair in the shower,
V is for Valerie who can pack a punch full of power.
W is for Wallace whose feet are very smelly,
X is for Xavier who blows bubbles in jelly.
Y is for Yvonne who pulls her friend's curl,
Z is for Zoe who's a perfect little girl!

Helen Rex (10)
Ravenbank Community Primary School

The Moon Haiku

Floating up above
Like a great big friendly face
Keeping me happy.

James Foreman (10)
Ravenbank Community Primary School

Rainbow

R ain falls and I appear
A bove everything large and small
I nsects, animals, people and buildings
N ow the rain has stopped
B efore I leave the sun comes out
O ver the clouds I rise and fall
W henever there is rain and shine I'll be there for sure!

Esme Shattock (10)
Ravenbank Community Primary School

Night

When I'm lying in my bed,
Thoughts running through my head,
I think about the night,
When it's not light or bright.
When I think about the stars,
They're not too far from Mars,
And the moon smiles at me,
And I fall asleep happily.

Harriet Morley (10)
Ravenbank Community Primary School

Mmmm! Chocolate!

Chocolate is the nicest thing,
You'll ever come to taste.
Even though our parents say
It's definitely not a waste.

Chocolate rules above them all,
Says the lady at the stall.
We wait around to be the first,
To eat Mars bars till we burst.

Peter Minaeian (11)
Ravenbank Community Primary School

My Mum, My Dad And My Cat

My name is Karina,
People ask, have you seen her,
Running around in her lilac hat,
Looking for Pepsi,
Her black and white cat?
I am average size,
But I wish I was higher,
The thing I like most,
Is singing with the choir.
When I get home from school,
I pester my daddy,
He does things for me,
Or I get 'saddy',
My dad helps me with my homework,
When I get stuck,
So then I can sit down
And read my book,
My cat sits beside me,
Purring with joy
Then jumps onto the floor
To find her toy.
Weekend is coming,
I will go to see Mummy,
Help her in the kitchen,
Rubbing my tummy,
Play with the children,
Running around,
Mum wants a snooze,
Sssh, don't make a sound,
This is my poem,
I've done my best,
My hand is now aching,
I need a rest.

Karina Schelze (10)
Ravenbank Community Primary School

My Cat Roxy

Roxy the cat is the first we've had,
She's as cute as a baby, but sometimes bad.
She's an acrobat, leaping on her toys,
Yowling and purring - she makes plenty of noise.
Life with her is fantastic and fun,
But if she eats much more, she'll weigh a ton!

Roxy curls like a snake, in her cosy bed,
Tail under her body, paws over her head.
When she wakes, she pounces on my feet,
Before she prowls around, searching for meat.
As I sit and stroke her silky soft fur,
I can't believe that we got her!

Laura Smyllie (11)
Ravenbank Community Primary School

The Breath Of The Wind

The wind has a terrible icy breath,
It crawls down my back like a needle through cloth.

It creeps down the street in a great mass of chill,
It roams around free at its own will.

The wind picks up leaves and hurls them around,
Then slowly they fall back to the ground.

But the wind gradually fades,
Through the hours of the day.

The reign of the sun has begun,
The time to play has come.

Christian Birchall (10)
Ravenbank Community Primary School

Light

Imagine the world without any light,
It would be even worse than losing a fight,
Darkness forever would be bad,
Lots of people would be very sad.

If there was a competition for need,
Light would be the number one seed,
So please sun don't go away,
Because people wouldn't be able to stay.

Mark Sarkar (10)
Ravenbank Community Primary School

Christmas Time

The faint reflection of the glittering moon
Twinkling on the frozen sparkling river.
The small, stiff leaves fall off the branches,
Into the frozen sparkling park river.

The crunchy white snow,
With a few fateful footsteps,
Leading to the warm houses
Where everyone is in front of the fire.

The sweet carol singers singing away
Getting louder and sweeter.
With their frozen papers
In the palm of their woolly gloves.

The fading stars glittering away
And the full moon as white as snow.
The wild winter dark night,
Whistling, 'Merry Christmas.'

Joshua Davenport (11)
St Ambrose RC Primary School, Adswood

The Donkey

In the play I'm a donkey
Not Joseph or Mary,
My fake ears are big
My coat itchy and hairy.

I wanted to be a king
But Miss said, 'No
You're safe as a donkey,'
Cried Miss Crow.

When Mary sits on me
It really hurts my back
So Mummy lined my coat
With an extra potato sack.

I didn't like my ears
Not at all,
So Miss Crow fixed them
So they weren't so tall.

On the big night
Mummy waved from her seat
My ears were in tact
And my coat was neat.

I fell and I cried
When I slipped on the mat
The play was ruined
And that was that.

'It's OK,' said Mum
When I sat on her lap
'You were the best in the show
And you got the biggest clap.'

Aislinn Walsh (10)
St Ambrose RC Primary School, Adswood

Mary In The School Play

I am Mary in the school play
I hold the baby that Sophie brought in
I wear some blue material
That my mummy had to find.

Sam is the donkey
I have to sit on him,
It is hard when I have the dress on
I have to toddle along with Joseph.

We have to find a place to stay
And plead with all our might
Then we have to go to a stable
And I sit on a chair in front of everyone
Rocking Sophie's baby.

I get lots of presents from the visitors
The Three Wise Men are there
Sarah is a Wise Man and her hat falls off
She carries on anyway and they give us the gifts.

The shepherds come with a lamb
And we stroke it
It is only a teddy
But the mummies and daddies don't know.

We have to take a bow
And we all hold hands
Our faces are bright red
We take another bow
And Sarah's hat falls off again!

Emma Downs (11)
St Ambrose RC Primary School, Adswood

A Window Christmas

When I looked out of my window,
I saw the sparkling moon,
The snow is falling all around,
As the carol singers sing in tune.

It is Christmas,
The tree is up,
Santa's sleigh sparkles,
Then Santa drinks out of our cup.

Winter footsteps crackling along,
Icicles on branches drip,
As the stars dance,
Santa makes his trip.

Jackie Battersby (11)
St Ambrose RC Primary School, Adswood

Winter Morn

Sparkling snow peppers the air,
The whispering, whipping wind dances,
The sun's soft glow peeps out from behind clouds,
The field is iced like a birthday cake.

Leaves of glass loiter on the ground,
Thousands of sharp spangly soldiers march over the plain,
Jack Frost has cast his wild frosty spell,
The trees sway their twinkling, silver arms.

Blankets of ice cover the ground,
Lakes glisten like pools of glass,
Twinkling lights sprinkle the houses,
That's what I saw through my window that morn.

Darcie Walsh (10)
St Ambrose RC Primary School, Adswood

British Cats

Cats, cats we're famous for cats
We love them all throughout the land
We pamper them from dawn till dusk
Cats, cats we're famous for cats.

Cats, cats we're famous for cats
We feed them freshly tinned food
We stroke them for two hours a day
Cats, cats we're famous for cats.

Cats, cats we're famous for cats
They purr softly while they sleep
Then in the morning they're ready to play
Cats, cats we're famous for cats!

Chlöe Farrow (10)
St Ambrose RC Primary School, Adswood

My Poem For Britain

The grand old houses beautiful in age,
Black and white timber and delicate glass,
Surrounded by lakes of glass and crisp green fields,
Deep enchanting forests with whispering trees.

The people who laughed there frolicked and played,
The grounds hold memories of past beautiful days,
Picnics, weddings, lunch or tea at the old hall,
The old house laughs at the delightful families.

Birds have flown past in the crystal-blue sky,
Creatures have lived in the deep undergrowths,
Children have played in the secret trees,
England is home to a beautiful history.

Darcie Walsh (10)
St Ambrose RC Primary School, Adswood

Summer

Summer is a fun time
People go on holiday
Red roses sweet with a perfume
Flower shops smell, sweet and sugary.

Bees hover around the yellow butter flower
Butterflies landing to take a deep breath and fly off
Ladybirds sit on the sweet green leaves
And munch, caterpillars spin a cocoon and go to sleep.

People begin to pack up their things
Off the beach and go home
Children tell their teacher
What a wonderful holiday they had.

Jessica Yates (10)
St Ambrose RC Primary School, Adswood

Anticipation Of Christmas

The cold winter wind flowed through the plaited,
Pointing fingers of the great oak tree,
The slow silver moon held high by the star-filled sky
Lingered over the frost-filled world.

Out of the window into the fog-filled night,
I could hear a lone dog howl into the night,
The iron earth under the thick fleece of snow,
That sparkled and glistened and was white with a glow,
With the carol singers singing softly in the snow,
Christmas was here.

Hannah Lawler (11)
St Ambrose RC Primary School, Adswood

My Dog

My dog can sing
He has got his own swing
He is called Jim
Jim is strong when he's at the gym
But he can be weak
And he's a good sneak
Most people think he's mean
But he just loves to clean
In the park
He will bark
Mostly people get scary
But he gets hairy
When he has a sniff
He will fall off a cliff
When he cleans the floor with a mop
He will not stop
He will get chased by a cop
And will hop
He robs the shop
He is crazy but not lazy
He is small
And has got his own ball
Jim went to the sugar shack
For a quick snack
He can get fat
But Jim will always chase the cat
He has big feet
And will always eat
Good old Jimmy.

Jacob Foster (9)
St Bede's RC Primary School, Weaverham

Summer

Summer is my favourite season,
Here is my special reason,
On a nice hot summer's day,
I go out to play,
If I am in the paddling pool,
I feel quite, quite cool,
The sun is shining bright,
What a lovely and wonderful sight,
When the ice cream man comes,
We are eating pieces of gum,
If you are on holiday on the beach,
In the sea there might just be a leech,
The heat is rising high,
Bigger than the warmest pie,
The butterfly is flying about,
Nicer than a boy scout,
All the flowers,
Need lots of showers,
And that is my special reason!

Georgia Hamnett (9)
St Bede's RC Primary School, Weaverham

Dogs

Playful puppies chasing cats,
Big dogs biting hats,
Fat ones, thin ones, tall ones, small ones,
Stealing the baker's buns,
Wet, cold noses,
Children cleaning dogs with hoses,
Glossy, colourful coats,
Thin, long, licky tongues.

Emily Pointon (9)
St Bede's RC Primary School, Weaverham

Friends

This is what we do today,
Just wake up and start to play.
'Hooray, this is Saturday.
Please, please, please, please can it stay?'

Now it's breakfast, time to eat,
We might have some delicious meat.
Oh goody good, we can have a sweet,
Sitting on a comfy seat.

Now it's time to ride our bikes,
We could go on a mountain hike.
Eeek! Look out, a giant spike,
We shouldn't have gone on this hike.

Now we're back, time for tea,
It's chicken nuggets for you and me.
Tomorrow we will go and ski,
Now we've eaten our scrumptious tea.

After tea it's time for bed,
Resting on pillows with our heads.
Night-night now is what we said,
Dreaming on, you sleepyhead.

Andrew Brown (9)
St Bede's RC Primary School, Weaverham

Kittens

Playful kittens
Wearing mittens
Sleeping on rugs
Chased by pugs
Playing with wool
They push and pull.

Rebecca Whittaker (9)
St Bede's RC Primary School, Weaverham

The Fingled Pingled Pig's Hat

There was once an animal called Fingled Pingled Pig,
Who had a hat the size of a fig,
All the animals wanted to live in his hat,
Apart from a really small owl called Pat.
There was not much room,
Not even for a bride or groom to go on their honeymoon.
One day he thought to himself,
Everybody wants to live in my hat, but it is too small,
If only it was the size of a big football.
Fingled Pingled Pig decided to buy a new hat from the shop,
So he set off in the rain, drip-drop, drip-drop,
He slowed down to stop in the shade,
Then a man came out and said, 'Want to trade?'
'Yes,' he said, 'can we trade that hat?'
His new one was big, wide and flat.
Now he walked back home,
All the animals stared, not one moaned,
He said, 'All you animals can live in my hat,'
Including the little owl Pat.
His hat was an animal hotel,
Much bigger than a motel.

Jonathan Stitch (9)
St Bede's RC Primary School, Weaverham

Pluto

Pluto has very long years,
So long they would give you fears.
Pluto is very cold,
And very, very old,
So I was told.
Pluto is so far from the sun,
You would not have much fun.

Molly Burrows (9)
St Bede's RC Primary School, Weaverham

My Feelings

I feel happy,
I feel sad,
Yesterday I went quite mad,
But also felt so sad.
The day before I didn't care
So I just sat down and ate my pear.
I feel down,
I feel like a sad clown,
Which makes me want to drown,
But then I really want to frown.

I feel angry,
I feel upset,
I am possessed,
About getting a pirate chest,
But my mate is the best.
I feel happy,
I feel glad,
Sometimes I get quite bad,
But the best way to cure it
Is to not get sad.

William O'Toole (9)
St Bede's RC Primary School, Weaverham

Pets

I've always wanted a cute, cuddly dog,
I will always find it in the fog,
I've always wanted a purring, pouncing cat,
I don't mind if it's fat,
I've always wanted a bouncing bunny rabbit,
When I come home from school I will pat it,
I've always wanted a humming hamster,
It won't be horrible like a gangster,
I've always wanted a heavy horse,
I will run it round the course.

Alice Jones (9)
St Bede's RC Primary School, Weaverham

Bullies

Bullies.
Scaredy-cats,
Jealous and cruel,
Sneering, like rats.
How would you like it
When at your school
It's made out
That you're a fool?
And it can't be nice
To go home at night
Knowing perfectly well what tomorrow held.
Another struggle, another fight.
Oh what a relief
When the weekend came.
Not a break from sums
But a break from pain.
Sometimes a fist, or maybe a kick,
Sometimes a mouth
That speaks and licks.
And the poor person
Receives blow after blow
Of all harsh words
The bullies know.
Those people really ought
To be ashamed,
For if you're a victim,
No sun, only rain.
Bullies.

Jodie Hughes (9)
St Bede's RC Primary School, Weaverham

The Sun Is Like . . .

The sun is like a little girl
Who sometimes wears diamonds and maybe a pearl
She always watches me
Above my big plum tree

The sun is like a little cat
Who sometimes prances and dances around her big blue mat
She always watches me
Above my big plum tree

The sun is like a little horse
Who sometimes gallops and canters around his obstacle course
He always watches me
Above my big plum tree.

Charlotte Owens (10)
St Bede's RC Primary School, Weaverham

Feelings

I feel happy, I feel sad,
I feel angry, I feel mad,
I feel anxious, I feel bad.

When I come home from school
Feelings rule,
But sometimes they are cruel.

When I'm at the farm,
I feel calm,
But not with an alarm.

When I'm in Spain
And I see the rain,
My feelings go down the drain.

Patrick Geoghegan Shaw (9)
St Bede's RC Primary School, Weaverham

Spring

Spring is the time when leaves grow back,
The birds fly by to have a snack.
It is the time when the sun is in the sky,
And your mum starts to bake a humble pie.
Little boys start to play football,
When tiny babies learn to crawl.
Spring is the time of love and joy,
And the kids start to annoy.
Now in spring children play,
And they nearly stay out all day.

Spring is the time when adults are in bed,
And they always have a cranky head.
No one's wearing woolly hats,
And the children start to play with cats.
Kids are out in shorts and T-shirts,
And the girls are wearing their mini skirts.
It's when the adults mow the lawn
And the toads start to lay frogspawn.
The birds are flying, the cats are scratching,
And the dogs are catching.

Aiden McTasney (9)
St Bede's RC Primary School, Weaverham

My Friends

Football is my friends' best game,
And they all want to be in some kind of fame,
They all love dogs,
And one of them got caught in a lot of fog.
They all have their doubts
About the horrible Brussels sprouts.

They are all very sporty,
And nowhere near forty,
They are all girlie,
And their hair is curly.

Georgina Shepherd (9)
St Bede's RC Primary School, Weaverham

Seasons

My favourite season is special spring,
Where the flowers come out to play.
The problem is, the bees join in and start to sting,
We play outside nearly all of the day.
That is my real reason of the special season.

The hottest season is significant summer,
Where we can play some sport.
The sun in the sky has just started to shimmer,
While families drive to their nearest airport.
That is my real reason of a significant season.

My worst season is awful autumn,
Where leaves spread their wings.
We also climb and get stuck in trees, so be cautious.
The leaves spread high onto a building.
That is my real reason of a spectacular season.

The coldest season is watery winter,
Where we can play in snow,
So wrap up tight Mr Finter,
And wear lots of socks for your toes.
That is my real reason of a shivery season.

Felicity Geary (9)
St Bede's RC Primary School, Weaverham

Dog

Slipper taker
Bone nicker
Cat runner
Butterfly chaser
Tail wagger
People licker
Hopping jumper.

Megan Pointon (9)
St Bede's RC Primary School, Weaverham

The Season Of Winter

Jumpers, scarves, woolly hats,
Frozen fur on chilly cats.
Lots of snow on big fir trees,
Cold children with wobbly knees.
Squirrels storing their food on high,
There are now not many clear blue skies.
Dancing, prancing, having fun,
Building snowmen with everyone.
Doing things without a care,
Smiles and laughter fills the air.
The ground is covered in a blanket of snow,
Standing outside you can't feel your toe.
Walking in the garden, makes your hands quiver,
It also makes your body shiver.
Lying by the fire, keeping warm,
Outside the window there could be a storm.
No leaves on the tree,
Its bark as slippy as can be.
When there are enormous, three-mile queues,
'Icy roads' it says on the news.
Icicles hanging from the windowpane,
Every year it's all the same.

Niamh Smith (9)
St Bede's RC Primary School, Weaverham

The Match

Twenty-six thousand came to the match today,
They queued and soon they will pay.
Crisps or hot dog,
Soon appeared fog
On the morning of Saturday.

All the crowd took up their seats,
My dad was the sneaky cheat,
So they kicked off the fabulous match,
What an unbelievable catch,
From the goalkeeper named McFleet.

He chucked it out to attack
And they hit it with a smack.
He shouted a call
And passed the ball,
But unfortunately hit his back.

Forty-five minutes have already gone,
Now they are back on.
The Scots are kicking off now,
But suddenly there was a row
Between the players. Then there were none.

So the crowd went down the stairs,
Fans just say, 'Who cares?'
So they got in their cars,
Driving home with the light of the stars,
But I bet they will have nightmares.

Christopher McNabb (9)
St Bede's RC Primary School, Weaverham

The River

See the river as it wanders
Like a long blue snake down the hill,
Weaving its way through towns and villages,
Past the boatyards, under the bridges,
Passing trees and houses.

Hear its quiet hiss as it slows down
To meet the sea,
See the kingfisher swooping down to catch his prey,
Only to escape for the next day.

Imagine the fish trying to escape
From the snake's huge mouth,
Suddenly, *snap!*
The kingfisher has caught another fish.

Alice Pointon (9)
St Bede's RC Primary School, Weaverham

What Is A Billion?

How many times have you wriggled your toes?
How many times has Homer Simpson been to Moe's?
How many hairs on your head?
How many bugs in your bed?
How many nights has the sun gone down?
How many trips have I made to town?
How many times have you eaten chips?
How many times have you licked your lips?

Matthew Burgess (9)
The Firs School

Seaside

As I look I see the . . .
Sea glistening as if diamonds
Had been sprinkled on top of it.
Sun shimmering like a glorious,
Glimmering, golden ball.
Ice cream man selling scrumptious,
Soft scoops of strawberry ice cream.
Waves crashing against shields of rocks.

As I sniff I smell the . . .
Salty smell of the sea.
A delicious picnic drifting towards my nose.

As I touch I feel the . . .
Sprinkly, soft sand in my toes.
A rough shell
And the suncream smooth on my skin.

Emily Cook (10)
The Firs School

If You Come

If you come to my house,
You will see a pink and furry mouse.
If you come to a sleepover you will hear a dog all night
That is shredding up a Barbie kite.
If you come on our walk,
You will see a parrot which will never squawk.
If you come in my bedroom you will see a tall
Daddy-long-legs climbing up my wall.
If you come into my garden you will hear a horse about to sing
In the cold and draughty wind.
If you come onto my drive,
You will have to cover up your eyes
And block your ears or else you will get an enormous shock
(And a big and nasty knock!)

Isobel Sherlock (9)
The Firs School

Rome

The capital city of Italy is Rome,
And it is a long, long way from home.

People go to St Peter's Square
Because they know the Pope will be there.

It's hot and sunny, no time to stop,
All day long you could shop, shop, shop.

The Colosseum is not all there,
But people still come to look and stare.

I sit and watch the Trevi Fountain,
While I eat an ice cream mountain.

Which kind of pizza? I can't decide,
When it comes, it's flat and wide.

Grazie, prego, buon giorno,
Arrivederci, it's time to go.

Georgia Cook (9)
The Firs School

Winter Through My Bedroom Window

As I sat in my bedroom all warm and safe, I gazed through my window,
The trees were bare, having been stripped of all their leaves by the
cruel winter weather.
The leaves had been left dead and scattered on the road below.
The branches now looked like bony fingers, with the wind passing
through them which made them appear to wave at me.
The roundabout on the hill sat still and lifeless,
The usual screams of laughter from the children could no longer
be heard.
You could see the rabbits peeping out of their holes to see the world
outside, whether it was safe.
As I looked I saw a dog run as fast as it could down the hill
like a cheetah.

Olivia Archer-Jones (10)
The Firs School

Thoughts On A Winter's Day

I wish the rain would go away,
I wish the sun would shine all day.
I wish it was as warm as toast,
I wish we could go to the coast.

I'm fed up with the wind and rain,
Drumming against the windowpane.
I'm fed up with the winter sky,
Of watching grey clouds scudding by.

But wait! The flowers need the rain,
To make them grow and bloom again.
The winter makes the snowdrops bloom,
The wind sweeps leaves up like a broom.

So welcome to the hail and snow,
That feeds the plants and makes them grow.
Winter, summer, autumn and spring,
Each season does its own gifts bring.

Jennifer Drummond (10)
The Firs School

Life In The Trenches (World War I 1914-1918)

The musky air is everywhere,
Sadness cannot stay inside one person's body, it spreads like
the plague.
Trying to look in the direction where home is looks so vague.
Smoke from the gunfire gets to your lungs, it has already killed four,
If any more die, we shall lose the war.
The rats don't care about the cold, they just want our flesh,
Getting home seems meaningless, trying to guess.
If we escape back to the ones we love, they will find us
And we all know the answer
Death.

Cassie Austin-Kaye (11)
The Firs School

Why?

Why am I grey every minute of the day?
Why have I got a long nose?
It spoils my pose.
Why have I got big ears?
They burst me into tears.
All sorts of things are wrong with me,
I wish I was the size of a bumblebee!
My mum thought I was a beautiful boy,
Her pride and joy.
But why?
Through my nose I make a chant.
After all, I am an elephant!
But why?
Bumblebees have got more colours,
That's not fair!

Alice Holden (10)
The Firs School

Animals Of The World!

They're green and yellow and pink and blue,
They're slippery, slimy, furry and new,
They're creepy, crawly, slimy, swirly,
And one of them is you.

They're super-duper, party pooper,
They're round and square and oval and air,
They're naughty, nasty, nice and neutral,
And that's a clue.

They live in the ocean, they live on the ground,
They can sing and run and twirl and pound.
They're straight and odd and funny and curled.
They're the animals of the world!

Georgina Holmes (11)
The Firs School

An Ode To Matilda

Roald Dahl's very clever girl,
Books never made Matilda's head twirl,
Books didn't make her have a worry,
Books didn't make her scream and scurry.
She read books as fast as a train,
But not quite as fast as an aeroplane!
She joined the library at the age of three,
Her thirst for knowledge was a joy to see,
For any teacher, especially Miss Honey,
Who was as kind as any teacher can be.
Matilda's parents were very mean,
They did not treat her as she should have been.
They also hated Matilda's guts,
Parents hating their children, they must be nuts!
Miss Honey loved Matilda so,
Together their love of books did grow.
Matilda's heart was full of hope,
Thinking would her parents want to cope
Without her living with them and TV,
For Matilda would then be free! *Be free!*
To let her dream come to reality,
Living with her darling Miss Honey!
This made both of their lives complete!
Best friends, good books, what an amazing feat . . .
For *Matilda!*

Maria Loizou (10)
The Firs School

Inside The Snake

Inside the snake was a tongue,
Inside the tongue was poison,
Inside the poison were tearful tears,
Inside the tears were awful memories,
Inside the memories were forests and leaves,
Inside the forests and leaves was a snake's mouth.

Camilla Bird (10)
The Firs School

Holiday Time

Playing in the garden on a swing,
Flying to the top of the tree.
Girlie giggles and screechy screams,
My sister on my knee.

Running down the path towards the beach,
Carrying my bucket and spade.
Building castles, mermaids and boats,
Then jumping on what I have made.

Packing the picnic in the bag,
Queuing at the zoo.
I wonder what we'll see today,
Elephant or kangaroo?

Walking in wellies and waterproofs,
Squelching in mud and water.
'Filthy trousers in the wash,
What a dirty daughter!'

Swimming up and down as fast as I can,
Diving into the pool.
It's hot outside in the sun,
What a brilliant way to be cool!

Sarah Willetts (9)
The Firs School

The Fox

Inside the fox's leg, there is a rabbit,
Inside the rabbit is fear,
Inside fear, the fox's teeth,
Inside the fox's teeth, the forest's howl,
Inside the forest's howl, the fox's bark,
Inside the fox's bark, there's the chase,
Inside the chase, there's death,
Inside death, the fox's leg.

Charlotte Graves (10)
The Firs School

Remembrance Day

November the eleventh,
All of the English army stand still,
No more shots of guns,
Explosions,
Shouts,
Screams,
Just silence.
In hospitals,
And trenches,
And villages,
And towns,
And tents.
People wondering,
What is going on?
Then they realise
And there are smiles
And laughter.
The war has stopped!
Eighty-five years from then,
Still on November the eleventh,
Remembrance Day is still here,
And there is a two-minute silence
To remember those who fought and died in the war.

Kitty Green (10)
The Firs School

The Rabbit

Inside the rabbit's heart, a generation,
Inside the generation, the fox's eye,
Inside the fox's eye there is a rabbit's frozen look,
Inside the rabbit's frozen look, there is death,
Inside death there is a rabbit's heart.

Zoe Duckworth (10)
The Firs School

With You

I cry at night for the little tap of a tree against the windowpane.
Times the tears go by again and again.

When I'm with him it's different, we go dancing on the sand.
Then I get my best dress on and we listen to the bands.

I'm bored on Sunday, chores which I can't stand,
But on Monday I just want to dance with her upon the land.

When I'm with him it's different, we go for picnics on the fields.
Then we chat for ages while we peel potatoes for the meals.

Then we dance at the banquets while everyone gazes in awe.
We dance and dance and dance until our feet are sore.

When we are together, everywhere we go,
We are always on show.

Amy O'Brien (10)
The Firs School

View

The fields are a patchwork quilt covered in lollipops,
The sky is a puddle with foam,
The fence is a row of CD cases,
It all looks a muddle.

The mud is one big toffee,
The grass is ripped green paper,
The sun is just a splattered egg,
It is just a picture to me!

The houses are blots of paint,
The road is a line of liquorice,
The street lights are golf sticks,
It is all so weird!

Katie Greenwood (11)
The Firs School

Amulet

Inside the zebra's mouth, the bitter taste of sand,
Inside the sand, a strand of zebra hair,
Inside the zebra hair, the tooth mark of a tiger,
Inside the tooth mark of a tiger, a zebra's blood,
Inside the zebra's blood, the zebra's mouth.

Catharine Verity (11)
The Firs School

Rhinos

Inside the rhino's horn is the vast savannah,
Inside the vast savannah, the rhino's hide,
Inside the rhino's hide is the sandy rock,
Inside the sandy rock, the rhino's sweat,
Inside the rhino's sweat is the oasis,
Inside the oasis, the rhino's eye,
Inside the rhino's eye is the circle of life,
Inside the circle of life, the rhino's horn.

Thomas Kerr (10)
The Firs School

Inside The Elephant

Inside the elephant there is an African plain,
Inside the African plain, there is an elephant's trunk,
Inside the trunk there is cool water,
Inside the cool water, there is an elephant.

Catherine Wood (10)
The Firs School

The Monster

The monster was as black as night
And as fearsome as death.
The monster was as tall as a skyscraper
And as fat as a pig.
The monster was as strong as ten oxen
And as sly as a fox.
The monster had a forked tongue like a snake
And feet like houses.
The monster's fangs were as sharp as knives
And as poisonous as snakes' venom.
The monster was so evil that Hell itself spat him out
And even the Devil feared him.
But rightly so for his cry made all feel like death
And none could restrain his will.

David Leyland (10)
The Firs School

The Curtain Of Mist

She was a bird on a silver carpet,
Balancing on wafers of thin steel,
Gliding on a mirror.

An eagle concentrating on its prey,
A kingfisher swooping onto its target.
Totally absorbed in a timeless waltz,
Closed from the outside world and all of its distractions.

A young bird on its maiden flight,
Reflected below in the curtain of mist.

Charlotte McNulty (11)
The Firs School

Football

Van Nistelrooy, he flew through the air like a jet,
The ball and his head, they met.
Into the back of the net it thundered,
How did he score that? I wondered.
The Southampton fans were whimpering,
And Van Nistelrooy, he was cheering,
He somersaulted down the pitch
And to the delight of the away fans, he fell in the dugout ditch.

Chris Simmons (11)
The Firs School

Lions

Inside the lion's mind, chase and slaughter,
Inside the chase and slaughter, the deer's leg,
Inside the deer's leg, the black thorn,
Inside the black thorn, the jungle forest,
Inside the jungle forest, the lion's mind.

Roseanna Yeoward (11)
The Firs School

Lion In The Wild

Inside the lion's paw, a golden plain,
Inside the golden plain, the lion's blood,
Inside the lion's blood, a stony cave,
Inside the stony cave, the lion's eye,
Inside the lion's eye, a waterhole,
Inside the waterhole, the lion's tongue,
Inside the lion's tongue, a sandy storm,
Inside the sandy storm, the lion's paw.

Lucy Smalley (10)
The Firs School

First World War

Goodbye love,
I'll miss you so,
Write lots,
Oh, please don't go!

Gas has been released,
Lots of people dying,
Hiding in the trenches,
Most people crying.

Lots of banging,
Children under the table,
I wish this could be
Some old fable.

Alice Walton (11)
The Firs School

Valentine's Day Shopping

I'm shopping around,
Nothing I've found,
What am I going to buy?

I think of his name,
It calls again,
And I stare stupidly at the sky!

I feel like I want to die,
I want to eat a pie,
Because I know he is the right guy!

Trini Woolley (10)
The Firs School

A Soldier's Poem

Guns on people's backs,
Grenades being thrown,
Gas masks being worn,
The king on his throne.
No one was safe
And people were on the chase.
It didn't end till 1918
And at that time I was nineteen,
But after that another started
And I fought until the end.

Daniel Ting (11)
The Firs School

Sarah Baxter

Sarah Baxter liked to shop,
She liked to dance
And she listened to pop,
A teenage girl
With her mind in a whirl,
Spending her money
Making her mum's hair curl.
On Saturday morning
She was up at ten
Phoning her friends,
'Coming round? But when?'
Off they would go
On the bus into town,
Not coming home
Until the sun went down.
She'd spend her money
'Oh no! There's nothing there!'
Her purse was empty,
Her purse was bare!
And that's how Sarah Baxter
Liked to shop, so there!

Emily York (8)
The Weaver Primary School

My Great Family

A family of five we are,
Parents, brother, sister, me and two posh cars.
As silly as we seem,
We follow a jolly theme.

We live in the countryside,
With trees and fields far and wide,
Our house is hidden out of sight
Which fills us up with sheer delight.

I love my family dearly,
I try to be good, well, nearly,
We all live here very happily
Which makes up my
'Great family'.

Harriet Tollafield (9)
The Weaver Primary School

The Sea

I stood upon the sands
Waving at the Chief of Waters,
He waved back at me
And so I wonder why,
Yesterday he tossed a boat upon the cliff
Turning its cargo to three dead bodies,
Why was he so angry,
And today so gay?
Perhaps he is confused
Or just very strange
That I shall never know
For he heads towards me
And I retreat up the steps,
Away from the Chief of Waters,
Away from the life-taker.

Alec Wilson (11)
The Weaver Primary school

The Bully

I am scared, please help me,
I'm being bullied at school,
You see them smoking cigarettes,
They think they are so cool.

It started in the dinner queue,
And look where it will end,
I've already been to hospital,
My friends are all too scared to defend.

I am scared, please help me,
I don't know what to do,
Shall I tell the teacher or,
Will she hurt me too?

I'm glad I told the teacher,
Everything is sorted out,
Because I didn't tell my mum,
I thought I would get a clout.

I am very happy now,
As I have moved away,
To a different school and house,
I have had a wonderful day.

But when I got back home from school,
My brother was in a state,
He was being bullied by my 2nd cousin's best mate.

Lianne Ingram (9)
The Weaver Primary School

I Love School

I love school, I think it rules!
We learn by using suitable tools.
Mrs Pierce is sometimes fierce,
We sometimes do maths and my class always laughs.
I love The Weaver School, I think it's really *cool!*

Daniel Harrison (8)
The Weaver Primary School

Teacher's Pet!

'Sit up Laura,
Be quiet Ben,
Use your ears Susie,
Sit up and then
Look this way
And listen to me,
No more chatting,
Come on Lee.

Come on Lily,
Look over there,
Look at Billy,
Sitting there.
He's not breaking any rule,
He's just . . .
Just such a jewel.
I do wish you were
All like that.'
'But Miss, Billy . . .
Is hiding a *rat!*'

Esther Richardson (9)
The Weaver Primary School

Cars

I love cars,
Sports cars, posh cars.
4x4s and long cars too.

The superb bodywork all shiny and new,
The sound of engines and roar of the exhaust.
The squealing of the tyres and screech of the brakes,
The thrill of the ride just makes me smile.

We speed along for mile after mile,
The scenery flashes by along the straights and round the bend.
I wish the ride would never end.

Ben Holland (8)
The Weaver Primary School

Muffin The Rabbit

My friendly rabbit called Muffin
Likes to run around all day,
She hops and jumps and skips
In a most unusual way.

She loves cabbages and carrots
For breakfast and tea
But loves Mum's plants, as you can see.

She digs amongst the garden
Burrowing here and there,
Under the fence and into next door
Which gives us all a great scare.

We chased her round the garden
To her great delight,
Until my sister Katie caught her in the night.

Home to her hutch,
To Sooty, her best friend,
My dad left with a fence to mend.

Tom Burt (9)
The Weaver Primary School

Football Mad

The ball hit the net
As the player scored.
The ball hit the net
As the rain poured.
The players cheered,
'Hurray, hurray!'
The players cheered,
What a lovely day.
The whistle went,
The start of fame.

Katie Steele (8)
The Weaver Primary School

A Viking Was Liking A Clock

Tick-tock, tick-tock,
A Viking was liking a clock.

Tick-tock, tick-tock,
A Viking was buying a clock.

But the ticks started tocking
And the cogs started knocking
A Viking was not liking this clock.

'I have no more!' said the man in the store,
'I am completely out of stock.'
A Viking was not buying this clock.

But just before he walked out the door,
He stopped and looked like a rock,
For right on time, the clock did chime
A Viking was buying this clock.

And every hour there was nothing as sour
As a bell, alarm or a dong,
Just the ticks that were tocking and the cogs that
Were knocking just like the notes of a song,
And a Viking was loving his clock.

Sophie Forster (8)
The Weaver Primary School

Cobra

I saw a cobra attacking my gerbil,
It attacked it wildly!
The cobra looked like the sky on a clear night.
It was too *slick* for any creature.
It dived at it continuously,
It tore it like paper,
The cobra is indestructible,
He will always win.

Ciaran Lunt
The Weaver Primary School

Cool Kids Of Class Six

C aitlin is competitive, cute but cunning,
L ianne is loud, lively but loving,
A ndrew is amusing, adventurous and able,
S am is smart, silly but stable,
S adie is small and she loves school,

S ome people are intelligent, some are cool and . . .
I n Class Six we don't have a master, we have Mrs Pierce with that
X factor.

Zoe Louise Conning (8)
The Weaver Primary School

The Robin's Season

Oh! Robin, Robin, with your breast so bright,
Shining in the snow,
such a beautiful sight.
In the spring
he loves to sing
in the shiny sunlight,
hopping and skipping through the grass,
looking for juicy worms for tea.

Sadie Bowen (8)
The Weaver Primary School

The Unicorn

A unicorn flies in the air like a white, soft cloud,
A unicorn's horn is like a sparkling star,
A unicorn's tail is like a beautiful firework,
A unicorn's face has style and grace as she flies past your place.
A unicorn's body is like a shining scaly fish,
A unicorn's feet are like a light
You can even see them shining in candlelight.
A unicorn's bum is like a seagull's wing swinging in the breeze.

Ashleigh Bampton (8)
The Weaver Primary School

Friends Forever

F riends are for fun!
R ound and round on the roundabout,
I n and out the tunnels below,
E very evening spent together,
N ever ever let each other go,
D own comes the rain, but doesn't stop us, no, no, no!

Tabatha Randle-Jones (9)
The Weaver Primary School

Adopt A dolphin

Whisky is cute, small and sweet: a smile to please everyone!
Nevis is talented, strong but good. Kindness and cuteness,
                                        that's Nevis!
Jigsaw's cool, she's such a big splasher! Friendly . . .
                                        amazing . . . wow!
Sutor is extra special, strong and brave, bravest of all!
Lightning is lightning, shocking . . . wow! exciting king!
Rainbow is beautiful, her beauty absolutely amazing.
Sundance is leader of the lot, strong, sophisticated, he's my guy!

Rommi Hulme (9)
The Weaver Primary School

Chocolate

C hocolate, chocolate,
H aving some fun!
O ld and brand new chocolate,
C overed in sweetness!
O lder kids love it,
L ayered in thickness,
A ll different names,
T earing all the wrappers,
E verybody loves it!

Joel Cotterell (8)
The Weaver Primary School

The Snow

The snow is white and icy too,
The flakes can fall on me and you.
Wrap up warm it's very cold,
It makes your face and nose glow.

Come on everybody, let's go outside,
Let's have fun and slip and slide.
Make a snowman round and fat,
Give him a nice woolly hat.

Emily Andersen (8)
The Weaver Primary School

All About Me

I'd love to be clever
but that's hardly ever.
I'd love to be quiet
but I usually cause a riot.

My hair is golden and frizzy
and long down to my back.
My teacher says I'm dizzy,
it's concentration that I lack.

Claudia Hamdy (8)
The Weaver Primary School

Ruby Rabbit

Ruby Rabbit jumps around her hutch,
Her small pink nose twitches so much,
She has long floppy ears and soft white paws,
With large buck teeth, a carrot she gnaws,
Running around with her tail like fluff
Like a little powder puff.

Sophie Hayes (8)
The Weaver Primary School

Up In The Sky

Up in the sky, birds sing,
Down on the ground, children play on a swing.

Under the sea, fish swim,
At the races, people win.

Up in the sky, aeroplanes fly,
Down on the ground, trees grow high.

Under the sea, seaweed sways,
All this happens while children play.

Matthew Beckley (8)
The Weaver Primary School

Dolphin

D arting in the waves,
O ver octopuses in the ocean
L ike mermaids in the deep,
P laying porpoise hide-and-seek,
H igh in the air like shadows dancing,
I n line with racing yachts,
N ever sad, always happy.

Morganne Shone (8)
The Weaver Primary School

Butterfly, Butterfly

Butterfly, butterfly, how far you fly,
You look so beautiful to the human eye.
You look so graceful when you land on a flower,
I could watch you hour by hour,
I watch you go from flower to flower,
You fly so peacefully in the morning sun.
I just wish we could have lots of fun.

Jade Corbin (8)
The Weaver Primary School

The Seaside

The sun is shining,
The sky is blue,
We are going to the seaside
With my friend, Sue.

We walk to the station
And wait for the train,
All the children singing,
We hope it will not rain.

The train pulls in,
We are on our way,
Sue and I shout,
'Hip, hip, hooray!'

We see the sand,
We see the sea,
All the exciting rides
As tall as can be.

Back to the station
Wait for the train,
The day is over
And it has started to rain.

Goodbye to the seaside,
Goodbye to it all,
We fall into bed
And say goodnight to you all.

Deanna Cartlidge (8)
The Weaver Primary School

This Is The Beach

Amber sands,
Crabs on land.

This is the beach.

Spiky shells,
Ice cream.

This is the beach.

Salty seas,
Waves go up and down.

This is the beach.

Coloured shells,
Seagulls screech.

This is the beach.

Children playing,
Parents asleep.

This is the beach.

Smelly seaweed,
Fish in the sea.

This is the beach.

I wish I could stay and play all day because

This is the beach.

Jemma Smith (8)
The Weaver Primary School

The Fish

The fish is multicoloured,
The fish is very cute,
My fish is a clownfish,
Its name is Nemo.

Nemo is a good swimmer,
Nemo is in my room,
My fish has two friends,
Their names are Spiky and Cho.

My fish speaks bubble language,
Nemo is my friend.
Nemo lives in a tank,
Nemo's friends are in the tank with Nemo.

Amy Walker (8)
The Weaver Primary School

Killers

A tiger can run very fast,
But racing a cheetah, he will come last.
Tigers love to come out at night,
If you meet him, he might give you a fright.

The crocodile is very snappy,
But with his children he is very happy.
The crocodile stalks buffalo;
He takes them on a death roll down below.

Polar bears are very scary,
Their big white coats are very hairy.
They're graceful swimmers in Arctic water,
And then they become experienced hunters.

Joshua Clive (8)
The Weaver Primary School

Snowing

S now is fun,
N ice and white,
O h what fun, a snowball fight.
W ithin hours it's all gone,
 I ce and cold follow on.
N ot nice now, snow's all gone,
G allons of slush left, that's no fun!

James Bailey (8)
The Weaver Primary School

Any Room Football

I like football,
I like it a lot,
I like to play it in the house,
But room I haven't got,
I dribbled round the table legs
And flew across the floor,
And scored a goal and hit a plate,
It was too late, it landed on the floor.
'Take it out, there's no room for it,'
Mum did shout!

Kerry Green (8)
The Weaver Primary School

Vikings

V ikings came to our shores
 I n longboats made out of wood,
 K ings to rule our lands,
 I nvading and plundering
N othing stood in their way,
G athering food, precious metals and gems,
S inging battle songs.

Luke Cockerton (8)
The Weaver Primary School

Our Holiday In The Motor Caravan
(To Grandma and Grandad)

Thank you for lending the caravan,
It was so very nice of you,
At first we went to Borth,
There were lots of things to do.

We went to Newquay and had our tea,
And then we went to bed,
It was so strange not being at home,
And so I cuddled up with Ted.

The very next day we could not stay,
So we went to the beach instead,
We saw lots of crabs, shells and fishes,
And seagulls that we fed.

It was so hot and we sweated a lot in Weston-Super-Mare,
We caught the train,
Had an ice cream
And then we went to the fair.

In Tenby we went to an Indian,
And had curry with some rice,
Katie thought that Tenby was really, really nice.

In St Ives we had a Chinese sweet and sour,
And when travelling home in the caravan
It took much longer than one hour.

Katie Rowland (8)
The Weaver Primary School

My Flute

My flute sounds like a beautiful, flying, quick, dancing fairy.
It sounds like a large, plodding, slow elephant.
My flute can be *loud* or quiet, also tuneful,
It can sound like swirling and blowing wind.
There are lots of keys, lots of notes,
My flute is shiny like the silvery moon.

Emma Wilmer (8)
The Weaver Primary School

In All Subjects!

Most people think literacy is boring,
And by the end of the lesson they will be . . .
Snoring!
In numeracy you have to concentrate,
For multiplying and dividing 2 and 8.
In art you'd better get a-moving and get things done,
Otherwise you will be behind *everyone!*
In music we play the drums,
And what's up? Yes! It's the thumbs.
In science there is hot and cold,
But please don't have to be told and told.
The Vikings are part of history,
They are people who travelled across the North Sea.

Kathryn Spiers-Pritchard (9)
The Weaver Primary School

Kittens

Kittens are cute
But can be very naughty indeed,
They drink, drink, drink,
And feed, feed, feed.
Kittens pounce over ornaments,
And bounce over the TV.
They crawl under the sofa
And sneak under the carpet.
Kittens are whirling balls of fur,
    Or
Slow, quiet, sneaking, black shadows.
They're just like kittens!

Lois Wylie (8)
The Weaver Primary School

Mum's Recipe

Nothing has been the same since Mum's recipe.
She won't play at all wit' you 'n' me.
You just wait 'n' see.
She doesn't wash, she doesn't clean and practically I think she's mean.
She won't even go to Kate when she's crying in her cot.
She thinks she's doin' a good job *but* she's *not!*
I miss Mum a lot.
Making Bakewell tarts, 'n' *never* playin' darts.
I can't wait till the day she says, *'Ready.'*
My whole family will be shouting *'Hurray for Mummy'*
But there is one thing I've got to admit,
Mum is *busy.*

Samuel Narici (9)
The Weaver Primary School

Names

People have such funny names
And also play some silly games.

Our names stay with us all of our lives,
Girls change their names when they become wives.

There're names of places
And we have different faces.

Without a name,
Things wouldn't be the same!

Oliver Tollafield (8)
The Weaver Primary School

Something Unseen

I've got a dream:
I watch it tenderly
In day as in night
But like water in a sieve
It all trickles tantalisingly away
Flying to another dreamer.

I've got a memory:
I keep it tentatively
Captive in my mind
But like a criminal in jail
It tries to break free into the world
And shocks me with its sudden disappearance

I have a secret:
I lock it up inside
My overcrowded head
Like the air in a balloon
It puts pressure on the inside
Finally it breaks out and is at last free.

Tom Young (11)
Tilston Parochial CE Primary School

Butterfly For Tea

A butterfly will flutter by,
As happy as can be.
But when it flies towards my mouth,
It ends up as my tea.

Christopher Duffy (9)
Tilston Parochial CE Primary School

Secrets

I'm thinking of my secret
like a dog I've just let off a lead
I run to catch it
but it still runs
I make a dive, I miss
but I will keep trying to catch it.

Rachel Jane Ewins (9)
Tilston Parochial CE Primary School

I Really Want A Dog

I really want a dog,
It sits there painfully,
Sorely in my heart,
Like a bubble that won't pop;
I hope Mum gives in
Before I scream.

Emma Ewins (11)
Tilston Parochial CE Primary School

My Secret

I think I have a secret,
A very private secret,
I have locked it up in the cave of my heart
And wrapped it up with bandages;
Like an Egyptian mummy in its tomb
But I know it will escape,
It will float down the River Nile;
Into the hands of someone else.

Alexandra Eleri Hunter (10)
Tilston Parochial CE Primary School

Power

I want power
So I can face my fears
I'm scared as hell
It's like a cat hiding from a dog
I'm too scared
Too scared to go outside.

Abby Cooper (11)
Tilston Parochial CE Primary School

Crossing The Road!

As the traffic roars past with
a wisp of a petrol aroma,
And lorries are rattling by with their
heavy loads and flapping sides.
We're trying to cross that herd
of beastly loud monsters.
Everyone can avoid being run over
by sticking to the Green Cross Code.
Stop, look and listen.

Jack Adie (9)
Tilston Parochial CE Primary School

My Secret

I've got a secret.
I carry it cautiously,
safely in my mind,
like Aztec gold,
in case someone finds out what it is
before I get rid of it.

Adam Flanagan (9)
Tilston Parochial CE Primary School

Antelope

Running on the plains, waiting until it rains.
The waterhole is dry.
They carry on with no water; it is as painful as slaughter.
With almost a tear in their eyes.
Running in a herd, the cry of the bird,
Means there's lions around.
They stop and stand still, the lion is ready to kill.
They do not make a sound.
The lion has a pounce, they scatter with a bounce.
Then comes the chase.
One is brought down, and there's silence all around.
It is a dangerous place.
But the antelope, just has to cope.

Hannah Rachel Littler (10)
Tilston Parochial CE Primary School

Inside My Dad's Head

Inside his head . . .
Memories of a happy childhood,
Hospital, bandage
Wedding day, and the bride
A lovely feeling inside.

Inside it you can see . . .
A framed picture just of me
Our old house
Rebecca as a toddler
And being served fish soup by a waiter called Klaus.

Inside his head is . . .
Winning the Olympic medal for the crawl
And meeting Anelka at a shopping mall
So now you know about my dad
Some thoughts are happy, some sad.

Lottie Brown (7)
Tyntesfield Primary School

The Sea

The sea is full with wonderful things,
With dolphins and fish with lots of wings!
Keep on swimming and swimming
You'll soon be singing!
Seashells and crabs,
But be careful, the crabs grab!
Well, that's it for now,
Look at that crab . . . *owww!*

Nicola Taylor (10)
Underwood West Junior School

Judo

Judo is the best
You throw people
And hold people down
At judo you have competitions
You can get in the north west team
At judo you go on trips and have gradings
That's why judo is the best.

Kelly Chedotal (10)
Underwood West Junior School

Monday's Dog

Monday's dog saves his bone
Tuesday's dog likes to be alone
Wednesday's dog likes to sleep in the house
Thursday's dog likes to chase the mouse
Friday's dog wears a hat
Saturday's dog likes to sit on the mat
But the dog that is born on the Sabbath day
Is pretty and rich in every way.

Kelsey Jade Shaw (9)
Underwood West Junior School

Please Mrs Cobb

(Based on 'Please Mrs Butler' by Allan Ahlberg)

'Please Mrs Cobb
This boy called Antty Patty
Keeps calling me names Miss
What should I do?'
'Go and sit in the hall, dear,
Go and sit outside dear,
Do what you want.'
'Please Mrs Cobb
This boy called Antty Patty
Keeps picking my rubber Miss
What should I do?'
'Go and work in the cupboard, dear
Do what you want
But don't ask me!'
'Please Mrs Cobb,'
'Go away, go away! Argh!'

Chantelle Butters (11)
Underwood West Junior School

My Secret Life Of Slumber

As I drift off from your imperfect Earth,
I can go places away from evil.
The night takes me places from my room,
Into a world where I am happy.
Away from hurt and my problems,
Everyone smiles and welcomes me.
I stand out in the crowd,
But when I am shook and shaken,
I realise I'm back on an imperfect Earth,
With my hurt and problems.

No one knows about my secret life
of slumber, just me!

Lauren Kaye (11)
Underwood West Junior School

At School We . . .

At school we . . .
At school we work.
At school we learn.
At school we run.
At school we play.
At school we exercise.
At school we write.
At school we colour.
At school we draw.
At school we divide.
At school we add.
At school we subtract.
At school we think.
At school we eat.
At school we times.
At school we paint.
At school we do literacy.

Robert Wardle (9)
Underwood West Junior School

My Pet Cat

I have a pet at home.
He sits all alone.
He is a pet cat.
He sleeps on a mat.
Felix Felix is his name.
I call him Fe Fe what a shame.
Every day he chases mice,
If he's lucky it may be twice.
He's a black cat,
Oh no he's asleep on my hat.

Paris Waller (9)
Underwood West Junior School

The Planet That Nobody Knew

There's a planet that scientists
Haven't found yet.
It hasn't got a name,
And it never will I bet.
So there it is yet all alone,
Nobody has settled
And made a home.
It is quite cosmic
A funky place,
The scientists haven't found it
And looked all round space.
I don't think they'll find it,
That proves they're not clever,
Because it's all made up,
The joke won't last forever!

Alice Brown (10)
Underwood West Junior School

Football Match

Henry passes the ball
Owen goes to score
Forlan goes for a fall
Beckham ignores the law
The referee saw
Pires is too tall
Half-time
Kewell is very fast
He's doing the weather forecast
Cole is on the ground
Why people are on the playground
Hunberg is Swiss
You are dismissed.

Anthony Steven Tweats (11)
Underwood West Junior School

Monday's Dog

Monday's dog is far too shaggy
Tuesday's dog is ever so waggy
Wednesday's dog wears a wig
Thursday's dog likes to dig
Friday's dog likes to bake
Saturday's dog loves the lake
But the dog that's born on the Sabbath day
Is wonderful in every way.

Emily Sproston (9)
Underwood West Junior School

Birthdays

Birthdays are great,
You eat lots of cake,

It's very yummy,
It's in my tummy,

Hip, hip, hooray,
It's my birthday today.

Alicia Hollinshead (9)
Underwood West Junior School

Happiness Is . . .

The summer holiday,
Playing with my Game Boy,
Swimming in the sea,
Playing with the dolphin,
Winning the gold FA Cup,
Flying to France.

Sam Crookham (11)
Underwood West Junior School

The Big Silver Moon

The moon shines like a silver spoon.
It shines like a car.
A rocket shoots up in the air
And loses his underwear.
Neil Armstrong lands on the moon.

Ryan Jones (9)
Underwood West Junior School

Dear Miss

(Based on 'Please Mrs Butler' by Allan Ahlberg)

'Dear Mrs Cobb,
This boy Joey Jew keeps hitting me
Miss what shall I do?'

'Go jump into the sea dear,
Go and write with ink,
Go swim with sharks my love,
Do whatever you think.'

Samantha Mason (10)
Underwood West Junior School

Alien Trouble

'Help, help! There's aliens about,
They're mean, they're green, they're ugly,
The laser guns are scary,
They live upon the red planet,
They come down on their spaceship
And capture all there is,
Help, help! There's aliens about!'

Dean Larvin (10)
Underwood West Junior School

The Train

(Slow)
Up a hill, finding it hard to do,
The engineer keeps on throwing coal in me.
I can't do this. Yes I can see the top
Nearly there, oh no!

(Fast)
At the top, need a rest.
Oh no! I'm stuck, can't move.
I'm thirsty, full up now.
Got to go, the engineer starts me up.

(Very fast)
Speeding down the hill at top speed
So fast I can't see anything.
Slowing down, nearly at the station
That's my nation. For kids my job's done.

Ashley Turner (10)
Underwood West Junior School

You

You
Your head is like a bounder
You
Your tongue is like a slimy snake
You
Your legs are like trees
You
Your hair is like long spaghetti
You
Your bum is like a hill.

Ryan Allen (10)
Underwood West Junior School

Monday's Dog

Monday's dog is far too stupid,
Tuesday's dog is as cute as Cupid.
Wednesday's dog is as greedy as some pigs.
Thursday's dog is at the digs.
Friday's dog is far too sleepy.
Saturday's dog is way too sneaky.
But the dog that is born on the Sabbath day
Is useless and lazy in every way.

Andrew Gorringe (8)
Underwood West Junior School

Summer

Summer, summer, bright and beautiful summer!
It makes me feel like dancing,
It makes the wind smell like roses.
Summer makes everyone happy but more than anything
It's my best season!

Lisa-Marie Beran (9)
Underwood West Junior School

Monday's Dog

Monday's dog is far too nasty
Tuesday's dog eats too much pasty
Wednesday's dog is a horrible sight
Thursday's dog will give you a fright
Friday's dog is far too raggy
Saturday's dog is far too shaggy
But the dog that is born on the Sabbath day
Is rich and pretty in every way.

Sean Aaron Reilly (8)
Underwood West Junior School

Monday's Dog

Monday's dog is far away,
Tuesday's dog is gong to pull Santa's sleigh,
Wednesday's dog is far too waggy,
Thursday's dog changes his name to Shaggy,
Friday's dog is such a pest,
Saturday's eats the rest,
But the dog that was born on the Sabbath day
Is pretty and perfect in every way.

Danielle O'Connor (8)
Underwood West Junior School

Monday's Dog

Monday's dog is quite big,
Tuesday's dog digs and digs,
Wednesday's dog is brown and white,
Thursday's dog flies a kite,
Friday's dog is ever so nice,
Saturday's dog has lots of lice,
But the dog who was born on the Sabbath day
Is good and nice, that's all to say!

Katie Hollinshead (8)
Underwood West Junior School

Monday's Dog

Monday's dog is very hairy,
Tuesday's dog is very scary,
Wednesday's dog is handsome and bright,
Thursday's dog gives a big, big fright,
Friday's dog is such a star,
Saturday's dog plays the guitar
And the dog that is born on the Sabbath day
Is rich and famous in every way.

Shannon Dowling (9)
Underwood West Junior School

Monday's Dog

Monday's dog is too shaggy,
Tuesday's dog is called Maggie,
Wednesday's dog is such a fright,
Thursday's dog howls in the night,
Friday's dog is cool,
Saturday's dog jumps in the pool,
But the dog that comes on the Sabbath day
Is pretty and perfect in every way.

James Woolrich (9)
Underwood West Junior School

Happiness Is . . .

When I am at school doing my work,
Playing with my friend at school,
On my birthday,
Clowns making me laugh,
Children playing on the street
Splashing in the puddles
And going to sleep with my teddy.

Sean Arnold (11)
Underwood West Junior School

Monday's Dog

Monday's dog is far too scruffy,
Tuesday's dog is lovely and fluffy,
Wednesday's dog is far too hairy,
Thursday's dog is like a fairy,
Friday's dog is always right,
Saturday's dog likes to fly a kite,
But the dog that comes on the Sabbath day,
Is the cutest dog in every way.

Kyle Wright (8)
Underwood West Junior School

Happiness Is . . .

The school holidays,
A new car,
Christmas time,
Getting pocket money,
Your birthday,
Playing with your friends,
Playing with leaves,
Going to bed,
Playing with my cars
And just having fun.

Adam Hopley (10)
Underwood West Junior School

I Wonder

I wonder, I wish I could be a big fish
Floating, fluttering, flying in the sea
The salty sea is the place for me.

Callan Holland (8)
Underwood West Junior School

You Are . . .

You are kind.
You are nice.
You're like butter.
You're so very nice.

You are naughty.
You are bad.
You are silly.
You are sad.

Amber Titterton (10)
Underwood West Junior School

From The Plane Window . . .

From the plane window I can see,
Fluffy clouds,
Birds flying in the sky,
Small buildings,
Small people,
Other planes,
Rain and lightning
And the big blue sky.

Kyle Scane (11)
Underwood West Junior School

Monday's Dog

Monday's dog is ever so small
Tuesday's dog is far too tall
Wednesday's dog is very clean
Thursday's dog is far too mean
Friday's dog is such a pest
Saturday's dog turns west
But the dog who is born on the Sabbath day
Will be cuddly and warm like the hay.

Lauren Astbury (8)
Underwood West Junior School

Monday's Dog

Monday's dog is far too fast.
Tuesday's dog is going to be last.
Wednesday's dog needs a rest.
Thursday's dog wears a vest.
Friday's dog is such a fright.
Saturday's dog is so bright.
But the dog that is born on the Sabbath day
Is the best in every way.

Nikki Cooke (8)
Underwood West Junior School

From My Car Window . . .

From my car window I can see . . .
A herd of cows,
An old man on a bike,
A big apple tree,
A fast motorbike
And a sheep.

Jason Purcell (10)
Underwood West Junior School

Monday's Dog

Monday's dog chases cats.
Tuesday's dog sits on mats.
Wednesday's dog is so mucky.
Thursday's dog is so scruffy.
Friday's dog catches rats.
Saturday's dog wears a hat.
But the dog that comes on the Sabbath day,
Is the best in every way.

Jessica Smith (9)
Underwood West Junior School

The Silver Moon

The moon shines like a silver spoon
It shines like a star
It spins like a car
A rocket shoots up in the air
And loses all the air
Neil Armstrong landed on the moon!

Kyle John Beech (10)
Underwood West Junior School

Monday's Dog

Monday's dog is far too sleepy,
Tuesday's dog is far too weepy.
Wednesday's dog is so hairy,
Thursday's dog is ever so scary.
Friday's dog is so fat.
Saturday's dog always chases a rat.
But the dog that is born on the Sabbath day
Is so fast in every single way.

Jack Roberts (9)
Underwood West Junior School

Happiness Is . . .

Happiness is . . .
When you go on holiday,
When you see your dad,
When you see your grandad,
When you go on a trip.

Aaron Beresford (11)
Underwood West Junior School

Monday's dog

Monday's dog is shaggy,
Tuesday's dog is raggy,
Wednesday's dog has his bone,
Thursday's dog is far from home,
Friday's dog has a rest,
Saturday's dog thinks he's the best,
But the dog that is born on the Sabbath day
Is rich in every way.

Abigail Lyn Murray (8)
Underwood West Junior School

And What A Storm!

And what a storm!
The world stood perfectly still and perfectly silent . . .
Then all of a sudden the storm crashed and banged
And screeched and rattled through the night.
The sky was as black as an evil witch's cat.
Thunder rattled and shook like a baby having a fit.
Wind pounced like a tiger chasing after its prey.
The lightning as bright as a lighthouse blazing across the sea.

Charlotte Nuttall (11)
Victoria Road Primary School

Red Is . . .

Bending down and hearing your pants rip.
A car waiting to go.
A lion chasing its prey on the second attempt.
A man bleeding in agony from an explosion.

Stephen Lawes
Victoria Road Primary School

And What A Storm!

And what a storm!
Noises calm and quiet rushing through the air.
The wind howled like a wolf howling at the moon.
Wind twisted and curled and looped.
Rain poured down like hailstones
Hitting the ground at its fastest speed.
Trees looking worried as the lightning shot down.
The lightning darted like a python's poison shooting into its prey.
Thunder bellowed and crashed and boomed.
Oh, what a night it was.

Sarah Rockliffe (11)
Victoria Road Primary School

And What A Storm!

And what a storm!
It was all silent.
Trees swirled and swished and whirled.
Then it went *bang!*
The rain blasted down
It was like a bucket of water pouring from the dark sky.

Brogan Ashley (10)
Victoria Road Primary School

What A Storm!

And what a storm!
The silence was as still as a tree.
The wild wind zoomed like a rocket passing through the Earth.
Thunder banged and roared
And shouted and screamed.
Lightning flashes like an adder slithering through the sky
To try and catch its prey.
The rain bounced down like a bouncy ball.
The stormy sky was as black as a blackboard.

Danielle Nickson (10)
Victoria Road Primary School

And What A Storm!

And what a storm!
The silence broke all noises.
The lightning struck
Like a person running in the dead of night.
A blow of wind howled like a wolf's cry.
Heavy downpours of rain pelted down
Like tumbling waterfalls.

Holly Davies (10)
Victoria Road Primary School

Red

Red is . . .
A bully being mean over and over again.
A fire burning in the hearth.
A song sung in front of a crowd.
A light halting the cars as the brakes hit the floor.

Michael Fryer (11)
Victoria Road Primary School

Black Is . . .

Black is . . .
Shadows running round me
Never taking their eyes off me.
Blindness surrounding me
With no way out.
A haunted castle ready to swallow me.
Poison running through me
Ready to kill.

Elly Campbell (10)
Victoria Road Primary School

Black Is . . .

Black is . . .
A haunted mansion with bats and demons inside.
A hand hurtling towards my face to punch me.
A mystery to solve with gruesome murders.
A coffin lowered into the ground in front of
Grief-stricken people sobbing.

Natalie Clutton (9)
Victoria Road Primary School

And What A Storm!

And what a storm!
Rain hit the floor like a gun shooting from the sky.
Trees cried and shut their eyes.
The clouds were like a load of bubble bath in water.
Thunder struck and burned the trees.
Trees fell like a bomb falling from a plane.
It carried on until it stopped . . .
There was silence.

Matthew Sanders (10)
Victoria Road Primary School

Red Is . . .

Red is . . .
A devil in Hell.
Going too near the fire.
A scar which my dad has on his knee.
A cut that is on any part of your body.

Adam Rockliffe (9)
Victoria Road Primary School

Black Is . . .

Black is . . .
The Devil hidden in the darkness with black piercing eyes,
Long fingernails and a screeching cry.

A person in a coffin covered with wood,
Sleeping forever without a sound.

Suffering from a broken arm
Making me scream, with my arm in plaster.

A haunted mansion with creaky doors,
Spiders crawling round and ghosts' footsteps on the ground.

Daisy Collins (9)
Victoria Road Primary School

What A Storm!

What a storm!
The rain boomed like a water bullet hitting the ground.
Flashes of lightning were hitting rocks
And making monster shapes in the dark.
It was raining cats and dogs.
The trees were holding up their hands in fear.
The wind was blowing making the trees look like scanty beggars
Against the midnight sky.

Amy Groome (9)
Victoria Road Primary School

What A Storm!

What a storm!
The thunder roared like a caged lion.
The lightning shot the sky.
There were frightening images of trees
That looked like monsters just waiting to destroy people.
There were scary shadows on the inner eye.
The wind battered the trees.
The rain poked the ground.

Kate Allman (9)
Victoria Road Primary School

What A Storm!

What a storm!
It crashed, rumbled, howled and smashed down trees.
The rain was like millions of tiny, little, pelting bullets
Shooting down from the sky.
The lightning flashed like electric eels.

Jack Kirkham (9)
Victoria Road Primary School

What A Storm!

What a storm!
It rumbled and crashed like bins banging to the ground.
The thunder sounded like bullets shooting around in the air.
Rain was teeming down.
Trees were blowing like scanty beggars in the storm.

Rebecca Lyon (9)
Victoria Road Primary School

The Mighty Beast

I stand at your mighty feet,
looking up at the sun sparkling on your icy top.
I will climb you. I will conquer you.
I accept your challenge.

I am climbing your beast, terrified of holes
In your wrinkled body.
Your hair hangs down over your face.
I will not give up.

I stand on your peak and I am on top of the world.
I feel really happy. I have won the battle.
I am the champion.

Ashley Smith (10)
Victoria Road Primary School

What A Storm!

What a storm!
The lightning was like a spear hitting the ground.
You could see the landscape
And the trees looked like monsters in the dark.
The rain was like a man punching the ground.

Stefan-Kevin Gallimore (10)
Victoria Road Primary School

What A Storm!

What a storm!
It banged like bombs exploding in the sky.
The rain howled like wolves.
The rain was like metal bullets punching the ground.
There were images of rocks and frightened trees,
Like scanty beggars in the wind.

Nikita McNulty (10)
Victoria Road Primary School

What A Storm!

What a storm!
The lightning flashes like a light switching on and off.
The sky is filled with sudden brightness.
The wind sounds like a wolf howling.
The rain drenches the whole world.
It is getting towards evening.
The trees hold their hands up in fear.
The gloomy fog gives people a shiver down their spine.
The image of trees and rocks look like shadows walking around.

Abbie-Leigh Jones (10)
Victoria Road Primary School

What A Storm!

What a storm!
The wind howled like a pack of wolves
Calling for help.
The thunder was like loud exploding bombs in the sky.
The lightning suddenly flashed in the sky,
Making the trees glow in the dark.

Thomas Turner (10)
Victoria Road Primary School

What A Storm!

What a storm!
The wind crashed like a shark rippling the flesh off its prey.
The wind was thrashing the trees about in dismay.
The lightning was crashing like a snake zigzagging in the sky.

David Alexander (11)
Victoria Road Primary School

What A Storm!

In a dark, gloomy forest the thunder exploded
With a mighty blast of sound in the sky.
The lightning was like one million speeding torpedoes
Coming straight at a target.
Whilst all that was happening,
Everywhere was getting drenched by the rain.
The wind roared like a whirlwind
And the dark trees were like old people rotting away.
The rocks were like crinkly brains on the ground.
The grass was like many Stanley knife blades
Shining in the moonlight.

Nathan Evans (10)
Victoria Road Primary School

What A Storm!

What a storm!
It rumbled and crashed like bins banging to the ground.
The thunder sounded like bullets shooting around in the air.
Rain was teeming down.
Trees were blowing like scanty beggars in the storm.

Melissa Ann Hough (10)
Victoria Road Primary School

What A Storm!

What a storm!
The thunder sounded like a bomb exploding.
The rain was coming down like a bomb.
The lightning looked like snakes speeding across the sky.
The rain was pouring to the ground.
The wind was rushing the trees down with a crash.

Lee Davies (9)
Victoria Road Primary School

What A Storm!

What a storm!
The rain was torrential.
It crashed against the trees.
The wind was as noisy as a pack of wolves
In the moonlight.
The thunder boomed like a cannon.
The lightning flashed
As bright as a thousand electric eels.
The trees looked like scanty beggars in the wind.

Connor Watson (9)
Victoria Road Primary School

What A Storm!

What a storm!
The wind howled like a dog.
The lightning flashes across the sky, zigzag like fire
The trees rattled like a bunch of rattlesnakes.
The train was punching the ground.
The moon was trying to give its light to the woods.

Zack McDonald (10)
Victoria Road Primary School

Red Is . . .

Red is . . .
A child diving into the deep end of the pool.
An oven cooking my special tea.
The brakes of my car as we enter a traffic jam.
A cut that I got opening an envelope.

Jonathan Bate (10)
Victoria Road Primary School

And What A Storm!

And what a storm!
Wind howled like a wolf.
Rain poured itself out of the evil clouds into the sea.
Clouds darkened the sky like a sheet rapping round the Earth.
Thunder bellowed over the evil killing sky.
Lightning struck the ground like a tiger pouncing on its prey.
Lighting ran through the evil clouds.
Trees petrified and damaged as the lightning struck them.

Stevie Stewart (9)
Victoria Road Primary School

Red Is . . .

Red is . . .
The shine in my eyes from a traffic light.
My tyres screech and I come to a halt.

An explosion about to blow up thousands
And thousands of buildings.

A cup of boiling hot chocolate running down my throat.

Seeing my team losing on a Saturday afternoon.

Luke Roberts (10)
Victoria Road Primary School

Yellow Is . . .

Yellow is . . .
A Honda Jordan F1 car speeding furiously.
An Egyptian sun scorching the people of Egypt.
A one pound coin being flipped.
A daffodil swaying in a calm breeze.

Fayad Uddin Choudhry (10)
Victoria Road Primary School

What A Storm!

What storm!
The rain is punching the ground rapidly.
The wind is winding everywhere.
The lightning is flashing so brightly you cannot see.
All that you can see are shadows of the naked trees.
Thunder is crashing and bashing.
Trees seem to give up in fear and dismay.

Daniel Ward (11)
Victoria Road Primary School

What A Storm!

What a storm!
It crashed and roared.
The wind battered against the window
Like a robber trying to break in.
Then the lightning filled the dark sky like a bright flame.
The thunder was like an explosion of dynamite.
The rain was pounding down on the soggy grass.
The trees held up their hands in fear.
The shadows were almost like monsters trying to capture their prey.

Steven Mulholland (10)
Victoria Road Primary School

What A Storm!

What a storm!
In a cold and dark forest
Thunder banged, roared and boomed.
The wind was howling like a pack of wolves
The trees were begging like scanty beggars
The shadows lying on the ground like monsters.

Elizabeth Parr (9)
Victoria Road Primary School

Red Is . . .

Red is . . .
A bull ready to charge.
A piece of chilli slipping
Slowly down my throat.
A crowd laughing at you
When you've just fallen over.
A car's brake screeching around the corner
Getting ready to stop.

Jenna McLean (9)
Victoria Road Primary School

Storm Poem

And what a storm!
The thunder growled and banged and crashed.
Trees' arms shook furiously
As though something evil was approaching.
The sound of the wind was like a black wolf growling over its prey.
Lightning lashed down like a shark darting through the sea.
And then silence!

Sam Evans (10)
Victoria Road Primary School

What A Storm

And what a storm!
The silence like a spooky bat flying around.
Wind twirled in the sky.
Thunder like a blizzard in the night sky.
Lightning flashed and flickered and blazed.
The rain was like a really light downpour from the sky.

Kirsty Purvis (10)
Victoria Road Primary School

Black Is . . .

Black is . . .
The Devil's evil smile.
The doom of someone living.
An old man next door facing death.
A lost baby in the dark and lonely streets.

Adam Malam (10)
Victoria Road Primary School

Black Is . . .

Black is . . .
A witch zooming through the night sky.
A dark alley letting no one pass its dark path.
A spooky haunted house which leads people to an evil way.
A devil's fire running through your spine.

Emma McCarthy (9)
Victoria Road Primary School

Red Is . . .

Red is . . .
A light telling you to let your clutch out on a motocross track.
A pitbull terrier pulverising someone's leg off.
A kite stuck on a pylon line.
Boiling hot chillies in my mouth.

Simon Morrall (10)
Victoria Road Primary School

What A Storm!

And what a storm!
The wind screeched like a bomb soaring through the sky.
The thunder crackled like burning flames from a fire.
Then it was silent like a cemetery at night.
The lightning flashed like an explosion in the night.

Tiffany Littlemore (10)
Victoria Road Primary School

And What A Storm!

And what a storm!
Silence grew over the dark and dusky town.
Lightning cut through the air like a sword
Piercing someone's heart.
Thunder crashed and banged and thumped.
Wind howled like a rabid pack of wolves.
Rain fell like birds beating on a window.

Ben Butler (10)
Victoria Road Primary School

Mount Everest

I stand at your feet,
Looking up at your powerful body
Feelings of excitement and amazement
Fill my body.
I can't wait to take your challenge.

As I begin to climb your face
I can feel myself getting more scared.
Your crevices look wrinkles.
You try and trick me with your avalanche.
But you don't fool me. I will defeat you.

I have now defeated you.
I now know I am on top of the world
I wish I could stay here but I know I can't.

Naomi Groome (11)
Victoria Road Primary School

The King Of All Mountains

I stand at your feet and tremble
You are gigantic with your powerful hands and body
Are you the king of all kings?
I will do this challenge whatever it takes
I slip and slide on your skin but the tricks are not working
I am at the top, I am over the moon
I am thrilled that I have survived
I am on the peak of the king of all mountains.

Ryan Histon (10)
Victoria Road Primary School

Mountain Of The World

I stand at your powerful feet.
Are you the king of all mountains?
I will climb you.
I will conquer you.
Get ready Everest for your defeat.

I climb up your mighty body.
Your icy hair falls but fails.
I am excited about climbing to your summit.
I am tired but I will not give up.

I am at the summit looking at the frosty view.
Some people tricked but not I.
I will never see your beautiful view of the world again.
I have defeated you Everest.
You will never forget this.

Christopher Birchall (11)
Victoria Road Primary School

What A Storm!

What a storm!
Images of trees like scanty beggars reach out
Like they are dying of hunger.
The wind sounds like a pack of wolves howling
And the lightning is like a big crack in the sky.
The trees look like monsters that have bones
And the thunder sounds like a hundred explosions
One after another.
The Earth is so dark
You can't see anything at all.

Daniel Quinton (9)
Victoria Road Primary School

On Top Of The World

I look up at your body. It is colossal.
Think of you as being an enormous giant.
Your head is like a majestic queen staring down.
Now I stand by your feet waiting to climb.
This is the greatest challenge ever.

As I start climbing you,
Your skin is so wrinkly.
I get nearer and nearer,
I can see your sparkling eyes.
Though the rain is starting to trick me,
I will still get to your face.

I stand on top of your head.
Now I can see your curly hair.
I am delighted that I conquered your body,
I am on top of the world.

Rachel Purvis (11)
Victoria Road Primary School

What A Storm!

What a storm!
The lightning bolts sparkled across the sky
Like a golden snake dashing through the grass.
The thunder exploded in the sky
Like an aeroplane crashing.
Wind echoed as loud as a wolf howling in the woods.
Would it ever stop?

Kimberley Hughes (9)
Victoria Road Primary School

What A Storm!

What a storm!
The storm crashed and rattled and creaked.
Thunder sounded like bins crashing down the street.
When the lightning flashed it looked like trees were begging.
There were gates creaking like wolves howling.
The wind screamed through the trees.

Victoria Smith (9)
Victoria Road Primary School

What A Storm!

What a storm!
The lightning rapidly flashed across the sky like an electric eel.
Wicked images of evil shadows moved across the rocks.
The rain shot across the sky like millions of watery bullets.
The wind was as noisy as a pack of wolves in the moonlight.

Andrew Donald (9)
Victoria Road Primary School

The Sleeping Cat

The sleeping cat calmly sleeps
In the shining moonlight.
There was not a peep at all, not a sound
Not even an owl hooting.
Suddenly it got up from the rugged pavement
And stretched his arms and legs,
But then it went away like a flash.

Richard Underwood (9)
Well Green Primary School

My Friends

I have friends
Just like you
We play together
Through the day
I enjoy it
So do you
We bounce and bounce
Through the town

We always go to the zoo
At half-past two
We love it
Just like you
We see all the animals
That's the best part
Then we go home
With you

We always stay together
At school
On school trips
And anywhere we go
We like everything
That we see
But the best thing
That we see
Is
You!

Ellie Armitage (8)
Well Green Primary School

The Magic Notes

Once there were some notes
some very odd notes that liked to sing, dance and prance
at night they loved to sing their favourite
song called 'I love notes'.

My owner plays the piano
so me and my best friend sing along to her practise
sheet so we sing and sing and sing!

And when we sing we dance and when we dance we prance.
I love to prance, dance and sing because that's our job,
so you can hear us sing a lovely song.

In my owner's book she's got all types, she's got sad, happy
And quiet ones, she's got loud ones too, she's got slow
And fast as well, my owner's the best person on Earth,
well . . . that's what me and my brother and sister think!

Penny Silverwood (9)
Well Green Primary School

My Dad!

My dad is a kind, gentle and playful dad
I love to play with my dad
My dad has a big heart
Full of love
I fit right inside with my mum and brother
I love the way my dad helps me
And gives up his time for me
My dad goes to work every day to make money for our family
My dad loves to watch the football
He also plays football
I love my dad!

Alice Gill (8)
Well Green Primary School

At The Seaside

At the seaside I can see crabs scuttling on the seashore
and children playing on the sand, that's what I can see.

At the seaside I can hear seagulls squawking in the summer
bright blue sky and the swishing sound of the sea
that's what I can hear.

At the seaside I can taste the lovely cold ice cream
melting on my tongue, after that I have minty sticky rock,
you know the stuff that sticks in your hair! That's what I can taste.

At the seaside I can smell the salty sea, hot chips
and sugary candyfloss, that's what I can smell.

At the seaside off come my shoes
And I can feel the hot sand running through my toes,
Across the pebbles and down to the beautiful sea.
That's what I can feel.

I just love all the seaside!

Alexandra Norbury (9)
Well Green Primary School

The Dragon

I saw a cloud like a dragon,
Lying in wait in the sky,
With a purple head and a purple tail
And a little blue patch for an eye.

From his snout came flames of fire,
And he began to run, chasing the daylight away
To the west and fighting the sun.

Savannah Walker-Ellis (9)
Well Green Primary School

The Veggie Lion

I am a veggie lion
I never never pounce
The first time I did so
I was thrown off, *bounce, bounce*

I am a veggie lion
I will be all my life
I was lurking in the forest
A hunter came by with a knife

I am a veggie lion
I nearly went to the zoo
I thought I would have to eat raw meat
I escaped at half-past two

I am a veggie lion
I discuss before I roar
I believe it's not correct
To break the lion law

I am a veggie lion
What is the great deal?
Mmm, fresh cabbages and carrots
Are my favourite meal

I am a veggie lion
My father is too
If you are a lion
Make you thoughts be *true.*

William Bundey (8)
Well Green Primary School

Sleepy Cat!

My cat was called Molly all day she dozed on the chair,
Nobody even knew she was there.
Except me, Jack, because she was my sleepy cat!
And it's as simple as that . . .

Jack Surplus (8)
Well Green Primary School

Kerry, Queen Of The Jungle

Kerry has won!
Now she is queen of the jungle.

Her blonde hair round her shoulders,
The grin across her face,
The tears in her eyes
As Ant and Dec told her the good news.
As Jennie showed her madness,
Kerry was swarmed with hugs.

She's had her fill of rice and beans.
She's faced her challenges like a heroine.
She's eaten ants and cockroaches too.
Yuck, yuck, yuck!
She did it, oh yes she did.

She just couldn't bare sixty thousand cockroaches
All over her face,
But she has won.

So three cheers for the queen of the jungle.

Lydia Smith (9)
Well Green Primary School

Our Loving Pets We Care For . . .

Do you love the pets that you care for?
If you do they should be like a friendly bunny to you
Cute and cuddly, your pussycat that crawls up
Your legs and goes 'miaow'.
Your hamster when it has chubby cheeks when it eats.
The obedient puppy that loves you.
Your lovely guinea pig that eats alone in the dark outside.
The dolphin with a beating heart and with a pointy nose.
Also a smooth, blue, shiny coat with water over it.

Olivia Papworth (9)
Well Green Primary School

Seasons

One spring morning the flowers began to grow.
One summer afternoon the sun began to glow.
One autumn evening the wind began to show . . .
But
One winter's night the snow began to fall
Every year it comes and goes
So let's see what next year brings!

Rebecca Jones (8)
Well Green Primary School

Friday Last Lesson

In the art room children drawing
Can't wait for the clock to strike,
Freedom, and when it does, sound of feet pounding
Chairs scraping and children laughing, fill the air as they go.

Inky fingers smudge the walls in the race to get
Their rucksacks they head for the gate
At great speed to be met by their parents.

Jack Lenihan-Smith (9)
Well Green Primary School

Who Am I?

Water splasher,
Wave crasher,
Dazzling diver,
Jazzy jumper,
Fish eater,
Coral stirrer,
Graceful swimmer,
Who am I?

Answer: dolphin.

Becky Niblett (10)
Winnington Park Primary School

What Am I?

They're as light as the breeze,
Higher than trees,
Softly and swiftly they creep.

They're as small as the bees,
Can travel with ease,
Softly and swiftly they creep.

They're as quiet as mice,
With wings like ice,
Softly and swiftly they creep.

They're as gentle as kittens,
With snowflakes for mittens,
Softly and swiftly they creep.

What are they?

Answer: fairies.

Madeleine Bullen (11)
Winnington Park Primary School

Children

C hildren are sweet and beautiful
H ave a good time and enjoy yourself
I ce cream are lovely in the heat
L ike a little child coming past you
D ays go beautiful
R eady just makes me fast
E very day I tell my day that I'm the one
N othing! But children are the best.

Rohini Solanki (9)
Winnington Park Primary School

The Laugh

When you're sat in class trying to concentrate,
Or an adult's about to shout,
By chance have you ever noticed,
That's when the laugh comes about?

'Cause it's all bottled up inside you,
Constant tickling inside of your chest,
For some reason your brain thinks it's funny,
And it *won't* just give up and rest.

You can try to ignore all its nagging,
But it forces a squirm and a wriggle,
In the end you give up and let it all out,
And it all starts off with a giggle.

So you see folks you don't always mean it,
But the laugh never does good to you,
Unless you can learn to control yourself,
A very hard thing to do!

Rachel Bousfield (9)
Winnington Park Primary School

Music

I love music, it rings in my ears,
I love music, it always appears,
In lots and lots of different ways, I see notes dancing on the page,
They swirl, then swing and whirl around,
Soon I'm humming, soon I'm singing, then I find myself
        dancing and twirling,
The time flies by and I'm ahead, how do I stop? Tell me, tell me how.

Kathryn Hooker (8)
Winnington Park Primary School

Stars

How do those shine so bright
And shine out with such might?
Flying like aeroplanes in the dead night,
Look up to them, wow what a sight!

Stars love to play around,
To hop, to skip and bound,
And do all this without a sound
And to see this wonder does not cost a pound.

So when you look up into the sky,
Just remember they can fly,
But just ask the question
Why do stars have to die?

Matthew Payne (11)
Winnington Park Primary School

Starlight

Streaks of silver shoot down
from the stars as they dance across the sky,
like a bullet from a gun of a man with a golden eye.

They twinkle like the lights
on a Christmas tree,
and shimmer like the sting of bees.

Stars make beautiful patterns in the sky,
especially when they are so high,
silver stars flicker and flash,
then they go dash, dash, dash.

Robyn Conway (10)
Winnington Park Primary School

Cats

Fat cats, thin cats, sitting on the bin cats,
Cats that bite, cats that fight
And cats that stay out all night.
Cats that play, and cats that stay
And cats that sit around all day!
Cats the clean, and cats the dream
And cats that lick up all the cream.

Cats that paw, cats that claw,
Cats that sit on the garden wall!
Cats that scratch, cats that hiss,
Cats that steal sausages from the dish!
Cats that miaow, cats that purr,
Cats that always clean their fur!

Vivien Ravenscroft (10)
Winnington Park Primary School

The Twix

I was eating a Twix while watching Vics
The ball being passed to and fro
'It's a goal,' they said cheering aloud.
As I jumped up and down, with the Twix in my hand.

As I sat back down, and lifted my hand,
The Twix was nowhere to be found.
The Twix had gone flying as I jumped
And that was the end of the Twix.

Sam Davey (11)
Winnington Park Primary School

In Winter

In winter, when the rain falls down,
People are out in the town,
While the strong gales are blowing around,
Soon it will start snowing, then you will hear the sound.

While the white snow whiffs away,
Children come out to play,
The moon screams out,
When everyone is dancing about,
The stars just twinkle around.

The moon sparkles in the shimmering sky,
While the sun goes in and says goodbye,
We will curl up into our bed,
I will rest my sleepy head.

Sarah Barclay (11)
Winnington Park Primary School

Snowy Day

S ilver flakes falling on the ground
N othing but glitter in the air
O ther people dancing and prancing on the ice
W inter has come and autumn has gone
Y oung and old enjoy the fun

D aylight has gone and the night draws in
A lways and forever we'll remember this day
Y esterday has passed which is when we had a blast and
                                      the future lies ahead.

Emma Brown (10)
Winnington Park Primary School

My Mum

My mum is fantastic.
My mum is sometimes irate.
My mum is angry and throws a binny.
My mum wakes up in a mood.
My mum thinks she owns the world.

My mum says, 'Go to school.'
My mum says, 'Where have you been?'
My mum is lazy and hangs around Scooby.
My mum watches telly and scoffs all night.
My mum goes to work and comes in at 5.30.
My mum thinks she's good and that's the end of the poem.

Tom Hewitt (11)
Winnington Park Primary School

Animal Kingdom

What was once a kingdom,
Is now very bare,
There is no life at all now,
Except the morning air.
There are no trees,
There are no bees,
There are no crispy autumn leaves,
The life has gone, we have surrendered,
There is no more of which we depended.

Abby Hardie (11)
Winnington Park Primary School

The Sun

The sun glows more than any of the planets and stars,
The sun is hotter than Mars and hot deserts.

The sun is made out of molten fire,
The sun surrounds the Earth with light.

The sun helps the stunning flowers and trees
And also helps the bees make the greatest honey.
The sun is the biggest flying ball.

The sun shines as bright as a beautiful shimmering diamond,
But when it shines brighter than before,
It might suddenly start to fall.

Zak Anderson (11)
Winnington Park Primary School

I Could Be . . .

I could be an astronaut
and float around in space.

I could be a doctor
and maybe operate.

I could be a post girl
and deliver you a letter.

I could be a vet
and make your pet feel better!

Annabel Johnson (10)
Winnington Park Primary School

Rainbow

R acing in the clear blue sky,
A ll the people cheer and cry,
I ndigo, red, violet, blue,
N ow which is the colour that would suit you?
B lack, white and maybe green,
O range and purple always to be seen,
W onderful colours glistening all day.

Siobhan Allmark (11)
Winnington Park Primary School

Mermaids

Mermaids are wonderful creatures.
Mermaids are kind to each other.
Mermaids are the best fishes that can make wishes.
Mermaids are the best of all the rest.
Mermaids are really pretty.

Rachael Ann Fryer (11)
Winnington Park Primary School

Teachers

Teachers are kind but sometimes frustrated,
Teachers are boring and sometimes creative.
Teachers dress smartly with shiny shoes,
Teachers are nice until they give rules.
Teachers read stories in the afternoon,
Teachers prepare us for the next school.

Amy Woakes (11)
Winnington Park Primary School

Guess Who?

Goal scorer
Cheeky diver
Arsenal cheater
Sometimes leader
Penalty winner
Football trainer
Free kick taker
Glove wearer
Battle winner

Who is it?

Answer: Pires.

Daniel East (10)
Winnington Park Primary School

Guess Who?

Water lover,
Snazzy swimmer,
Jazzy jumper,
Dazzling diver,
Lovely leaper,
Mega mover,
Slick learner,
Perfect performer,
Ocean winner.

What am I?
A dolphin.

Lauren Randles (11)
Winnington Park Primary School